SPELLING

essentials

for the Pre-GED Student

Laurie Rozakis, Ph.D

THOMSON
★
ARCO

Australia • Canada • Mexico • Singapore • Spain • United Kingdom • United States

An ARCO Book

ARCO is a registered trademark of Thomson Learning, Inc., and is used herein under license by Peterson's.

About The Thomson Corporation and Peterson's

The Thomson Corporation, with 2002 revenues of $7.8 billion, is a global leader in providing integrated information solutions to business and professional customers. The Corporation's common shares are listed on the Toronto and New York stock exchanges (TSX: TOC; NYSE: TOC). Its learning businesses and brands serve the needs of individuals, learning institutions, corporations, and government agencies with products and services for both traditional and distributed learning. Peterson's (www.petersons.com) is a leading provider of education information and advice, with books and online resources focusing on education search, test preparation, and financial aid. Its Web site offers searchable databases and interactive tools for contacting educational institutions, online practice tests and instruction, and planning tools for securing financial aid. Peterson's serves 110 million education consumers annually.

For more information, contact Peterson's, 2000 Lenox Drive, Lawrenceville, NJ 08648; 800-338-3282; or find us on the World Wide Web at: www.petersons.com/about

Acknowledgments

Much thanks to my wonderful editor, Wallie Walker Hammond. Wallie, you're every writer's dream editor: intelligent, perceptive, and kind. It's always a pleasure working with you!

ISBN: 0-7689-1245-8

Printed in the United States of America

10 9 8 7 6 5 4 3 2 1   05 04 03

First Edition

Contents

Section IV   Putting the Words Together

Section V   Words Commonly Confused

Section VI   Reevaluating Your Skills

Section VII   Appendices

Introduction

You are taking a big step toward success on your GED test. You have a full, busy life, and we know that you want a test-prep book that gives you fast and easy access to the skills that you need. We've created *Spelling Essentials for the Pre-GED Student* with that in mind.

These days, there are people who think that spelling is not very important. They argue that since most people use a computer to write, they can just use the spell checker. Well, a spell checker can't help you when you have to fill out a job application. The fact is, you're *judged* on your spelling. Also, misspelling a lot of words in a document may prevent you from relaying clear and accurate information.

This book will teach you some simple spelling rules and word parts that will make spelling a lot easier for you. Soon you'll have much more confidence when it comes to your writing. It *is* worth the effort to learn to spell!

About This Book

First, you're going to take the Pretest. The Pretest will help you figure out what you need to focus on. The book is then divided into four review sections:

- Fundamentals of Spelling
- Spelling Rules
- Putting the Words Together
- Words Commonly Confused

Each of these sections will teach you the spelling skills that you will need to prepare for the GED tests, including:

- Vowel and consonant sounds

- Silent letters

- Contractions and possessive nouns

- Plural nouns

- Prefixes and suffixes

- Words often misspelled

You'll also work with practice spelling drills or "quick quizzes" in the review sections. For additional practice, you'll find a "Practice Test" at the end of each chapter right after the answers for the quick quizzes. After working through all of these review sections, you should take the Posttest to see how much you have learned. Finally, we've included some test-taking tips and strategies in the Appendix to help you out on your GED test day.

By the time you're finished, you'll be so confident in your abilities to spell correctly, you won't need that computer spell checker!

Let's get started.

Evaluating Your Skills

Pretest

Take this mini pretest to help you understand where you are strong and where you need to practice.

Directions: In each of the following groups of words, only **one** of the words is misspelled. Choose the misspelled word and spell it correctly on the lines provided for you.

_____ **1.** shiny   potatoe   knives   shepherd

_____ **2.** baggy   cieling   canine   vengeful

_____ **3.** contagious   obituary   lonliness   transferable

_____ **4.** sacrafice   caramel   burglarize   veterinarian

_____ **5.** publicity   sieze   patriarch   wiry

_____ **6.** bridle   loosely   breakage   symtom

_____ **7.** apologetic   truancy   diploma   surpise

_____ **8.** uncanny   statuesque   aisle   familair

_____ **9.** Artic   trigonometry   exhaust   visualize

_____ **10.** vegatable   ceiling   colleague   probably

_____ **11.** dissaprove   fiend   diagnosis   magnificent

_____ **12.** original   bravely   mispell   incidentally

_____ **13.** sking   almond   vocal   friendliness

_____ **14.** wholly   Britian   exercise   president

_____ **15.** conceled   wholesome   witness   certain

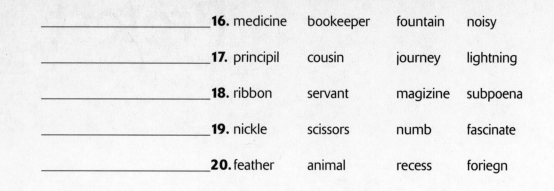

	16. medicine	bookeeper	fountain	noisy
	17. principil	cousin	journey	lightning
	18. ribbon	servant	magizine	subpoena
	19. nickle	scissors	numb	fascinate
	20. feather	animal	recess	foriegn

Answers

1. potato

2. ceiling

3. loneliness

4. sacrifice

5. seize

6. symptom

7. surprise

8. familiar

9. Arctic

10. vegetable

11. disapprove

12. misspell

13. skiing

14. Britain

15. concealed

16. bookkeeper

17. principal, principle

18. magazine

19. nickel

20. foreign

Fundamentals of Spelling

Vowel Sounds 1

Vowels and Consonants

English has twenty-six (26) letters and twenty-one (21) of the letters are called **consonants.** The consonants are:

b	c	d	f	g	h	j	k	l	m	n
p	q	r	s	t	v	w	x	y	z	

Five (5) of the letters are called **vowels.** The vowels are:

a   e   i   o   u   y (sometimes)

Sometimes, *y* sounds like a vowel. For example: *bye.* Here, the *y* sounds like an *i.*

Quick Quiz A

Directions: In the spaces below, write **C** if the letter is a *consonant.* Write **V** if the letter is a *vowel.*

_____ **1.** c   _____ **6.** o

_____ **2.** l   _____ **7.** w

_____ **3.** p   _____ **8.** a

_____ **4.** u   _____ **9.** r

_____ **5.** h   _____ **10.** m

Quick Quiz B

Directions: In the space provided, write the vowels:

_____   _____   _____   _____   _____

and sometimes _____

Syllables

Every word is made up of one or more *syllables*. A syllable contains one or more letters and each syllable has one vowel sound. The vowel sound may be formed by two or more vowels, as long as the vowels work together to make one sound. Here are some examples:

Number of Syllables	Examples	Word Divided into Syllables
1 syllable	peace	peace
	meat	meat
2 syllables	maybe	may be
	penny	pen ny
3 syllables	together	to ge ther
	anymore	a ny more
4 syllables	independent	in de pen dent
	declaration	de clar a tion

Knowing how to sound out syllables can help you figure out how to spell and say long words. If your first language is Spanish, we'll give you some hints later on as they relate to Spanish pronunciations.

Quick Quiz C

Directions: In the spaces below, write the number of syllables in each word.

_____**1.** surprise   _____**6.** orange

_____**2.** education   _____**7.** cow

_____**3.** box   _____**8.** late

_____**4.** photograph   _____**9.** hospital

_____**5.** journey   _____**10.** dandelion

Now, let's look at the vowel sounds to discover how they are spelled in English. Slash marks / / are used in this book to set off the symbols that are used to show sounds. The slash marks are there to remind you that they're not letters or words.

Sounds

The Short /a/, /e/, and /i/ Sounds

Here are some examples:

/a/ as in *hat*	/e/ as in *red*	/i/ as in *pig*
brand	sell	skin
track	rent	think
damp	shell	thing
fact	shelf	quit

Understanding the difference between the vowel sounds in *hit*, *hot*, and *hut* may be difficult for you if English is not your first language. Practice saying and spelling these word groups:

sit / sock / sun

tip / top / tug

nick / not / nut

The Short /o/ and /u/ Sounds

/o/ as in *fox*	/o/ as in *dog*
fond	loss
rock	off

/u/ as in *bus*	/u/ as in *bush*, *push*, and *brush*
dust	oo as in *book*, *look*, and *took*
bump	ou as in *could*, *should*, and *would*

The Long /a/ Sound

In this sound, the vowel says its name: The /a/ sound is pronounced like *ay*.

/a/ as in *cake*	/a/ as in *sail*	/a/ in *tray*
lake	main	hay
late	nail	bay
laser	chain	stay

Take a look back at the *ai* combination in the middle row at the bottom of page 9. Notice that you have two vowels in a row: *a* and *i*. But only the first vowel, *a*, is heard. You can remember this by using a little rhyme:

"When two vowels go walking, the first does the talking."

In this case, the *a* and the *i* are walking together. The *a* is first, so that's the sound you hear. However, you will need to remember to include both vowels when you spell the word!

The Long /e/ Sound

/e/ as in *beet*	/e/ as in *seal*
weed	heat
greet	cream
queen	bean

The Long /i/ Sound

/i/ as in *lime*	/i/ as in *kind*
time	grind
bite	pint
line	find

/i/ as in *fly*	/i/ as in *pie*
try	lie
shy	tie
fry	die

If Spanish is your first language, use this hint to help you spell words with the long /e/ sound: The long /e/ sound in English is similar to the sound of the letter *i* in Spanish, as in *libro* (book).

Quick Quiz D

Directions: Circle the correct word to complete each sentence.

1. The (heet, heat) feels good.
2. Do you have the (bok, book)?
3. The (leef, leaf) turned red.
4. The bird flew (eway, away).
5. Nik takes the (buse, bus) to work.
6. I got something in my (eye, eey).
7. Kids like ice (creem, cream).
8. The child is (afraid, afrad) of the dark.
9. We swim in the (lake, laik).
10. Juan is (shy, shi).

The Long /o/ Sound

/o/ as in *cold*	/o/ as in *bone*
colt	stone
smoke	vote
hold	cone

/o/ as in *roast*	/o/ as in *show*
toast	show
loaf	bow
coast	flown

The /o/ Sound

/o/ as in *ball*	/o/ as in *haunt*
stall	sauce
false	haul
small	fault

/o/ as in *fawn*	/o/ as in *fought*	/o/ as in *daughter*
dawn	bought	taught
raw	thought	caught
law	ought	sausage

The /u/ Sounds

The sound /ur/ as in *herd* and *turn* does not exist in some languages. If English is not your first language, you might want to practice this sound by saying and spelling the following words: *herd*, *turn*, *girl*, and *worm*.

/u/ as in *cute*	/u/ as in *moon*
tune	soon
cube	smooth
use	tooth

/u/ as in *news*	/u/ as in *blue*
blew	glue
stew	true
chew	clue

Quick Quiz E

Directions: Choose the word that is not spelled correctly. Spell it correctly on the lines provided for you.

_____	1.	use	smok
_____	2.	raw	nauhty
_____	3.	falce	lawn
_____	4.	ago	lof
_____	5.	chew	toul
_____	6.	vot	below
_____	7.	even	droup
_____	8.	law	schol
_____	9.	toste	drew
_____	10.	busy	sause

The /ou/ and /oi/ Sounds

The English sound /ou/ is like the sound of the letters *au* in Spanish, as in *aula* (classroom). The English sound /oi/ is like the sound of the letters *oy* in Spanish, as in *hoy* (today).

/ou/ as in *couch*	/ou/ as in *cow*
cloud	crowd
mouth	growl

/oi/ as in *boil*	/oi/ as in *boy*
spoil	joy
coin	toy

The /ar/ Sounds

The sound /ar/ in English is similar to the letters *ar* in Spanish, as in *caro* (expensive).

/ar/ as in *star*	/ar/ as in *dare*	/ar/ as in *pair*
card	square	stair
mark	stare	hair
smart	bare	chair

Quick Quiz F

Directions: Some of the following words are misspelled. Write **C** if the word is spelled correctly and write **X** if the word is spelled incorrectly. Then spell the misspelled words correctly on the lines provided for you.

_____**1.** clowd

_____**2.** mowth

_____**3.** croud

_____**4.** growl

_____**5.** chare

_____**6.** smart

_____**7.** coin

_____**8.** stare

_____**9.** sqare

_____**10.** spoile

Write the misspelled words correctly:

_____   _____

_____   _____

_____   _____

The Final /ē/ Sound

A two-syllable word may end with the /ē/ sound.

/ē/ as in *penny*	/ē/ as in *turkey*
study	donkey
navy	hockey
twenty	chimney

Answers to Quick Quizzes

Answers to Quick Quiz A

<u> C </u> **1.** c

<u> C </u> **2.** l

<u> C </u> **3.** p

<u> V </u> **4.** u

<u> C </u> **5.** h

<u> V </u> **6.** o

<u> C </u> **7.** w

<u> V </u> **8.** a

<u> C </u> **9.** r

<u> C </u> **10.** m

Answers to Quick Quiz B

a, e, i, o, u, and sometimes *y.*

Answers to Quick Quiz C

<u> 2 </u> **1.** sur prise

<u> 4 </u> **2.** ed u ca tion

<u> 1 </u> **3.** box

<u> 3 </u> **4.** pho to graph

<u> 2 </u> **5.** jour ney

<u> 2 </u> **6.** or ange

<u> 1 </u> **7.** cow

<u> 1 </u> **8.** late

<u> 3 </u> **9.** hos pi tal

<u> 4 </u> **10.** dan de li on

Answers to Quick Quiz D

1. heat

2. book

3. leaf

4. away

5. bus

6. eye

7. cream

8. afraid

9. lake

10. shy

Answers to Quick Quiz E

1. smoke

2. naughty

3. false

4. loaf

5. tool

6. vote

7. droop

8. school

9. toast

10. sauce

Answers to Quick Quiz F

___X___ **1.** clowd

___X___ **2.** mowth

___X___ **3.** croud

___C___ **4.** growl

___X___ **5.** chare

___C___ **6.** smart

___C___ **7.** coin

___C___ **8.** stare

___X___ **9.** sqare

___X___ **10.** spoile

Misspelled Words Corrected

1. cloud

2. mouth

3. crowd

5. chair

9. square

10. spoil

Practice Test

Directions: Circle the word that is misspelled in each line. Then spell it correctly on the lines provided for you.

_____**1.** studie   penny

_____**2.** late   animore

_____**3.** hospitel   cow

_____**4.** donkee   rent

_____**5.** brand   sause

_____**6.** surprise   oringe

_____**7.** peece   hay

_____**8.** gloo   main

_____**9.** maybe   thouht

_____**10.** qeen   thing

Answers

1. study
2. anymore
3. hospital
4. donkey
5. sauce
6. orange
7. peace
8. glue
9. thought
10. queen

Consonant Sounds 2

As you learned in Chapter 1, twenty-one (21) of the letters are called **consonants.** Take another look at the consonants below to refresh your memory:

b   c   d   f   g   h   j   k   l   m   n

p   q   r   s   t   v   w   x   y   z

Some of the consonants are used on their own. Others are used in pairs or groups of three to make English spelling patterns.

The Soft /g/ or /j/ Sounds

The letter *g* usually stands for the sound you hear at the beginning of *goat* or the end of *bug*. This is called the *hard g* sound.

Sometimes *g* is followed by *e*, *i*, or *y*. Then it stands for the sound you hear at the beginning of *gem* and at the end of *cage*. This is called the *soft g* sound. The letters *dge* also create the soft *g* sound. Here are some examples:

/g/ as in *gentle*	/j/ as in *jug*	/j/ as in *ledge*
cage	jam	bridge
sponge	joke	wedge
range	jar	edge

Quick Quiz A

Directions: Circle the word in each pair with the *soft g* sound.

1. giant   glimmer
2. gem   glass
3. gym   glee
4. stage   bug
5. age   gift
6. page   hug
7. bridge   plug
8. badge   flag
9. large   goat
10. cage   jug

The /s/ Sounds

The /s/ sound is also very important in English spelling. It can be spelled three different ways: *s*, *c*, and *ss*. You will never see *ss* at the beginning of a word in English. It appears in the middle or end of a word.

/s/ as in *sad*	/s/ as in *mice*	/s/ as in *grass*
same	cell	dessert
sink	rice	cross
soap	twice	tossed

Letter Blends

The /skr/, /spr/, /skw/ Sounds

Sometimes, three letters stand for a sound that is blended together. The letters *scr*, *spr*, and *squ* are three examples. You have to listen carefully to hear all three letters, and sometimes it is hard to do so. That is why it is very helpful to learn these letter patterns. Knowing these three letter blends will help you spell many useful words correctly.

/skr/ as in *scrape*	/spr/ as in *spring*	/skw/ as in *squirrel*
screen	spray	squeal
scream	sprain	squeak
scramble	spread	squint

Quick Quiz B

Directions: Circle the three consonants in each word that combine to make one sound. Look for the letters *scr*, *spr*, and *squ*. Then write each word twice. This will help you remember it.

1. scratch _____ _____

2. screwdriver _____ _____

3. sprig _____ _____

4. screen _____ _____

5. scribble _____ _____

6. sprint _____ _____

7. squirm _____ _____

8. sprawl _____ _____

9. squish _____ _____

10. sprain _____ _____

The /ch/ Sound

/Ch/ is another common English sound. The spelling pattern for this sound is *ch* or *tch*.

Ch is often at the beginning or middle of a word. *Tch* does not appear in the beginning of any English word. It is only used in the middle or at the end of a word.

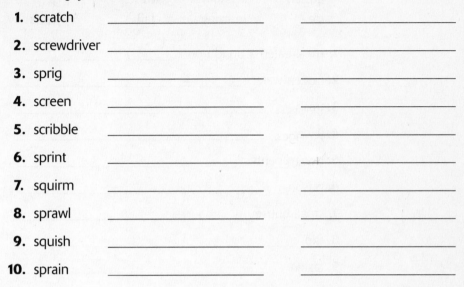

/ch/ as in *much*	/ch/ as in *itch*
which	catch
witch	scratch
speech	watch

Quick Quiz C

Directions: Write the spelling word that matches each definition on the lines provided for you. Use the words in the box as your guide.

attach	scissors	lunch	gem	garbage
ice	journey	jail	jeans	cottage

1. meal eaten around noon _____

2. frozen water _____

3. trash _____

4. jewel _____

5. denim pants _____

6. prison _____

7. small house _____

8. trip _____

9. fasten _____

10. cutting tool _____

The /f/ and /k/ Sounds

The /f/ sound can be spelled *gh* or *f*.

/f/ as in *rough*	/f/ as in *phone*	/k/ as in *stalk*
tough	phrase	talk
cough	graph	yolk
wrought	typhoon	chalk

The /m/ Sound

/m/ as in *drum*	/m/ as in *lamb*
worm	crumb
sum	thumbnail
steam	climb

Quick Quiz D

Directions: Match each misspelled word to its correct spelling. Write the letter of the correct spelling on the lines provided for you.

Misspelled Words	*Words Spelled Correctly*
_____ **1.** wurm	**a.** unless
_____ **2.** combb	**b.** talk
_____ **3.** clim	**c.** chalk
_____ **4.** crum	**d.** worm
_____ **5.** tawk	**e.** yolk
_____ **6.** thumnail	**f.** comb
_____ **7.** yowk	**g.** laughter
_____ **8.** luaghter	**h.** crumb
_____ **9.** unles	**i.** climb
_____ **10.** chawk	**j.** thumbnail

The /n/ and /r/ Sounds

/n/ as in *knee*	/n/ as in *sign*	/r/ as in *wrong*
know	gnat	wrote
kneecap	gnaw	wreck
knit	signature	wristwatch

Quick Quiz E

Directions: Sort the following words into the correct groups, by their consonant sounds.

graph	phone	knit	phony	knight	knockout	typhoon	know

/f/ spelled *ph*	/n/ spelled *kn*
_____	_____
_____	_____
_____	_____
_____	_____

The /wh/ Sound

The letters *wh* together stand for the sound you hear at the beginning of words like *white* and *when*. Here are some other examples:

	the /wh/ sound	
whistle	why	where
while	whispered	wheat

The /z/ and /zh/ Sounds

/z/ as in *please*	/z/ as in *zoo*	/z/ as in *fuzz*
cheese	freeze	buzzer
usual	zero	jazz

/zh/ as in *treasure*	/zh/ as in *garage*
measure	beige
pleasure	mirage

Quick Quiz F

Directions: Some of the following words are misspelled. Write **C** if the word is spelled correctly and write **X** if the word is spelled incorrectly. Then write the misspelled words correctly on the lines provided for you:

_____**1.** wistle   _____**6.** weat

_____**2.** while   _____**7.** meazure

_____**3.** cheeze   _____**8.** jazz

_____**4.** please   _____**9.** where

_____**5.** freese   _____**10.** garaje

Write the misspelled words correctly:

_____   _____

_____   _____

_____   _____

Words with Double Consonants

Some words with two syllables have a double consonant in the middle of the word. The double consonant is two letters, but together they make one sound. You cannot always hear the vowel, so you have to study these words carefully.

Double *l*	Double *p*	Double *s*	Double *n*	Double *r*
allow	happen	lesson	cannot	carrot
scallop	happy	blossom	cannon	errand

Quick Quiz G

Directions: Circle the double consonant in each of the following words. Then write the word three times on the lines provided. This will help you remember how to spell it.

1. parrot _____ _____ _____

2. occur _____ _____ _____

3. button _____ _____ _____

4. puzzle _____ _____ _____

5. missile _____ _____ _____

6. balloon _____ _____ _____

7. cotton _____ _____ _____

8. ballad _____ _____ _____

9. rattle _____ _____ _____

10. lettuce _____ _____ _____

Answers to the Quick Quizzes

Answers to Quick Quiz A

The first word in each pair has the *soft g* sound.

Answers to Quick Quiz B

1. (scr)atch
2. (scr)ewdriver
3. (spr)ig
4. (scr)een
5. (scr)ibble
6. (spr)int
7. (squ)irm
8. (spr)awl
9. (squ)ish
10. (spr)ain

Answers to Quick Quiz C

1. lunch
2. ice
3. garbage
4. gem
5. jeans
6. jail
7. cottage
8. journey
9. attach
10. scissors

Answers to Quick Quiz D

1. d

2. f

3. i

4. h

5. b

6. j

7. e

8. g

9. a

10. c

Answers to Quick Quiz E

/f/ spelled *ph*	/n/ spelled *kn* as in *knee*
phony	knight
typhoon	knockout
phone	knit
graph	know

Answers to Quick Quiz F

__X__ **1.** wistle   __X__ **6.** weat

__C__ **2.** while   __X__ **7.** meazure

__X__ **3.** cheese   __C__ **8.** jazz

__C__ **4.** please   __C__ **9.** where

__X__ **5.** freese   __X__ **10.** garaje

Misspelled Words Corrected

1. whistle

3. cheese

5. freeze

6. wheat

7. measure

10. garage

Answers to Quick Quiz G

1. pa ⟨rr⟩ ot

2. o ⟨cc⟩ ur

3. bu ⟨tt⟩ on

4. pu ⟨zz⟩ le

5. mi ⟨ss⟩ ile

6. ba ⟨ll⟩ oon

7. co ⟨tt⟩ on

8. ba ⟨ll⟩ ad

9. ra ⟨tt⟩ le

10. le ⟨tt⟩ uce

Practice Test

Directions: Some of the following words are misspelled. Write **C** if the word is spelled correctly and write **X** if the word is spelled incorrectly. Then write the misspelled words correctly on the lines provided for you.

_____**1.** ocurr   _____**7.** sprain

_____**2.** watch   _____**8.** zeroe

_____**3.** coff   _____**9.** brige

_____**4.** scramble   _____**10.** pleasure

_____**5.** talk   _____**11.** sponje

_____**6.** clim   _____**12.** which

Write the misspelled words correctly:

_____   _____

_____   _____

_____   _____

Answers

___X___ **1.** ocurr   ___C___ **7.** sprain

___C___ **2.** watch   ___X___ **8.** zeroe

___X___ **3.** coff   ___X___ **9.** brige

___C___ **4.** scramble   ___C___ **10.** pleasure

___C___ **5.** talk   ___X___ **11.** sponje

___X___ **6.** clim   ___C___ **12.** which

Misspelled Words Corrected

1. occur

3. cough

6. climb

8. zero

9. bridge

11. sponge

Silent Letters 3

You may have learned to spell words by sounding out all the letters. Sometimes that *is* a good way to spell English words. Other times, however, it will not work. Why? Because many English words have *silent letters*. In this chapter, you will learn how to spell words with silent letters.

Silent letters are part of the word, but they are not said. Even though the letters are not said, you still have to include them in the spelling of the word. Here are two examples:

- half   The *l* is silent.   The word is said: *HAF*
- thumb   The *b* is silent.   The word is said: *THUM*

The Silent *b*

The *b* can be silent at the end of a word or in the middle of a word.

- comb   The *b* is silent.   The word is said: *KOME*
- plumber   The *b* is silent.   The word is said: *PLUM-er*

Below are ten words with a silent *b*. Read the words aloud:

crumbs	limb
dumb	debt
thumb	doubt
subpoena	comb
subtle	climb

Quick Quiz A

Directions: Circle the correct word to complete each sentence.

1. If you spend more than you earn, you go into (dett, debt).
2. It is hard to (climb, clime) that big mountain.
3. Something that is not easy to see is (suble, subtle).
4. The dog licked up the (crumbs, crums).
5. The tree (limb, limm) fell on the house.
6. No one likes being called (dumm, dumb).
7. The lawyer gave the thief a (subpoena, supoena).
8. I (dout, doubt) I can get to the train on time.
9. The baseball pitcher broke her (thumb, thumm).
10. Rita fixed her hair with a (comm, comb).

The Silent c

The silent *c* can be hard to find because the *c* tends to blend into the word. Don't be tricked! Below are the most-often used words that contain the silent *c*:

acquaint	acquire	acquit	fascinate
muscle	descend	scent	scissors

The Silent g

English has many words with a silent *g*. Since they are used often, you'll need to know how to spell them. Here are some of the most common ones:

design	gnaw	sign	campaign
resign	reign	foreign	align

Quick Quiz B

Directions: Match each misspelled word to its correct spelling. Write the letter of the correct spelling on the lines provided for you:

_____ **1.** desine   **a.** gnaw

_____ **2.** siggn   **b.** campaign

_____ **3.** resin   **c.** design

_____ **4.** forin   **d.** foreign

_____ **5.** campain   **e.** sign

_____ **6.** aline   **f.** align

_____ **7.** reing   **g.** resign

_____ **8.** naw   **h.** reign

The Silent *gh*

As you have already discovered, the *gh* pattern is common in English words. The words below all have a silent *gh*:

ought	fought	brought
bought	rough	eight
freight	right	slight
delight	fright	copyright

Quick Quiz C

Directions: Write each of the following words three times on the lines provided for you. This will help you remember how to spell them.

1. delight _____ _____ _____

2. freight _____ _____ _____

3. ought _____ _____ _____

4. eight _____ _____ _____

5. fought _____ _____ _____

6. copyright _____ _____ _____

7. brought _____ _____ _____

8. right _____ _____ _____

9. slight _____ _____ _____

10. fright _____ _____ _____

11. rough _____ _____ _____

12. bought _____ _____ _____

The Silent *h*

Rhyme and *rhythm* are often misspelled because of their silent *h*. Here are some more words with a silent *h*:

ghost	spaghetti	shepherd	exhaust
vehicle	heir	herb	exhibit

Quick Quiz D

Directions: Spell each of the following words correctly on the lines provided for you. The silent *h* may be missing or it may be in the wrong place in the word.

1. sheperd _____

2. veicle _____

3. spagetti _____

4. exaust _____

5. eir _____

6. erb _____

7. exibit _____

8. gost _____

The Silent *k*

Words with a silent *k* are easier to spell if you remember this hint: Look for words with the *kn* combination. Here are some of the most common ones:

knock   knack   knoll

knob   knives   know

Quick Quiz E

Directions: Circle the silent *k* in each of the following words.

1. knoll

2. knack

3. knives

4. know

5. knob

6. knock

The Silent *l*

Words with a silent *l* fall into two groups or patterns: *alm* or *no alm*.

alm pattern	*no alm* pattern
palm	talk
almond	walk
salmon	stalk
balm	would
calm	folk
	half
	folklore

Quick Quiz F

Directions: Sort the words in the box with a silent *l* into two groups: Those with the *alm* pattern and those without it. Write the words on the lines provided for you. Then circle the *alm* or silent *l* in each word.

half	salmon	would	folklore
talk	palm	folk	almond
walk	calm	stalk	balm

alm pattern	*no alm* pattern
_____	_____
_____	_____
_____	_____
_____	_____
_____	_____
_____	_____

The Silent *n*

Again, look for patterns. The silent *n* is found most often at the end of a word, as these four examples show below:

autumn   hymn   column   solemn

The Silent *p*

The silent *p* is very hard to find because it can be in the beginning, middle, or end of a word. Study this chart for more practice:

silent *p* in the beginning	silent *p* in the middle	silent *p* at the end
psalm	cupboard	receipt
pneumonia	raspberry	corps (the *s* is silent, too)
psychology	empty	

Quick Quiz G

Directions: Write the correct spelling of each word on the lines provided for you. Look for a silent *n* or a silent *p*. The silent *n or p* may be missing or it may be in the wrong place in the word.

1. emty _____

2. colum _____

3. autum _____

4. cuboard _____

5. salm _____

6. hym _____

7. receit _____

8. sychology _____

The Silent *s*

The silent *s* is sneaky like a snake! It can be anywhere in a word. Here are some examples:

island   debris   aisle   Louisville

The Silent *t*

Several important words have a silent *t*. Here are the words you will often use in your everyday writing:

listen   stretch   wrestle   bankrupt

whistle   Christmas   mustn't   mortgage

Quick Quiz H

Directions: Circle the silent *t* in each of these words:

1. whistle
2. stretch
3. listen
4. wrestle
5. Christmas
6. mustn't
7. mortgage
8. bankrupt

The Silent *u*

Most words with a silent *u* have a partner: A silent *g*. Look for the *gu* pattern. Here are some examples:

guess	guest	guide
guarantee	bodyguard	lifeguard

The Silent *w*

Here are words with a silent *w*:

answer	sword	wrap	whose
wrought	whole	wreath	two

Answers to the Quick Quizzes

Answers to Quick Quiz A

1. debt
2. climb
3. subtle
4. crumbs
5. limb
6. dumb
7. subpoena
8. doubt
9. thumb
10. comb

Answers to Quick Quiz B

1. c
2. e
3. g
4. d
5. b
6. f
7. h
8. a

Answers to Quick Quiz D

1. shepherd
2. vehicle
3. spaghetti
4. exhaust
5. heir
6. herb
7. exhibit
8. ghost

Answers to Quick Quiz F

alm pattern	no *alm* pattern
p<u>al</u>m	ta<u>l</u>k
<u>al</u>mond	wa<u>l</u>k
s<u>a</u>lmon	fo<u>l</u>klore
b<u>al</u>m	wou<u>l</u>d
c<u>al</u>m	fo<u>l</u>k
	ha<u>l</u>f
	sta<u>l</u>k

Answers to Quick Quiz G

1. empty

2. column

3. autumn

4. cupboard

5. psalm

6. hymn

7. receipt

8. psychology

Answers to Quick Quiz H

1. whis(t)le

2. stre(t)ch

3. lis(t)en

4. wres(t)le

5. Chris(t)mas

6. mus(t)n't

7. mor(t)gage

8. bankrup(t)

Practice Test

Directions: Some of the following words are misspelled. Write **C** if the word is spelled correctly and write **X** if the word is spelled incorrectly. Then write the misspelled words correctly on the lines provided for you.

_____**1.** delight

_____**2.** rough

_____**3.** bodyguard

_____**4.** eihgt

_____**5.** thum

_____**6.** plumber

_____**7.** muscle

_____**8.** fright

_____**9.** spahetti

_____**10.** forein

_____**11.** rihgt

_____**12.** desin

_____**13.** empty

_____**14.** guide

Write the misspelled words correctly:

_____   _____

_____   _____

_____   _____

Directions: Circle the word that is misspelled. Then write it correctly on the lines provided for you.

15. crumbs   anser   _____

16. subpoena   dout   _____

17. thum   scissors   _____

18. doubt   iland   _____

19. libm   guest   _____

20. dum   answer   _____

21. comb   Chrismas   _____

22. autum   climb   _____

23. giude   debt   _____

24. mucsle   subtle   _____

Answers

   <u>C</u> **1.** delight

   <u>C</u> **2.** rough

   <u>C</u> **3.** bodyguard

   <u>X</u> **4.** eihgt

   <u>X</u> **5.** thum

   <u>C</u> **6.** plumber

   <u>C</u> **7.** muscle

   <u>C</u> **8.** fright

   <u>X</u> **9.** spahetti

   <u>X</u> **10.** forein

   <u>X</u> **11.** rihgt

   <u>X</u> **12.** desin

   <u>C</u> **13.** empty

   <u>C</u> **14.** guide

Misspelled Words Corrected

4. eight

5. thumb

9. spaghetti

10. foreign

11. right

12. design

15. answer

16. doubt

17. thumb

18. island

19. limb

20. dumb

21. Christmas

22. autumn

23. guide

24. muscle

Oddball Words 4

When you see the spelling of a word in a dictionary, you are seeing its *phonetic* spelling. For example, the word *phonetic* would be shown as follows:

(foe *neh* tik)

In the *phonetic alphabet*, letters and symbols stand for the sound of the word as you say it. In Chapters 1 and 2, you learned that many words can be spelled by the way they sound. For example, you learned that the long /e¤/ sound is spelled *ee* as in *beet* and *ea* as in *seal*.

Unfortunately, some English words don't sound the way they are spelled. As a result, these oddball words are difficult to spell.

The following exercise can help you learn how to spell difficult words, such as ones that are not spelled the way that they sound. Follow this list below:

1. Say the word. Use it in a sentence.

2. Get a mental picture of the word, syllable by syllable. Say the letters in order.

3. Close your eyes and spell the word.

4. Write the word. Check your answer.

5. Write the word five to ten times.

In addition to these study tips, there are some ways we can group oddball words to make them easier to remember how to spell. Let's look at these groupings now.

Words that Have a *Y* Where You Expect an *I*

Below is a list of words that sound like they have an *i*. Instead, each one of these words has a *y* that creates the *i* sound:

analyze	anonymous
cylinder	cynical
hypocrisy	paralysis
syllable	synonym
sympathy	symphony

Quick Quiz A

Directions: Add a *y* to complete each of the following words.

1. s__mpathy

2. c__nical

3. paral__sis

4. h__pocrisy

5. anal__ze

6. s__llable

7. s__mphony

8. s__nonym

9. c__linder

10. anon__mous

Words with Oddball Endings

The following words are difficult to spell because they don't end the way they sound:

1. Words that end in *-ar* (but sound like they should end in *-er*):

beggar	burglar	cellar
bursar	calendar	liar

2. Words that end in *-ain* (but sound like they should end in *-in*):

Britain	captain	certain	chieftain
curtain	mountain	porcelain	villain

3. Words that end in *-cian* (but sound like they should end in *-tion*):

There is an easy way to remember this. End the word with *-cian* (rather than *-tion*) if you can trace the word back to a word that ends in *-ic*. Here are some examples:

-ic word	*-cian word*
electric	electrician
music	musician
pediatric	pediatrician
politic	politician
mathematics	mathematician
optic	optician
physic	physician
statistic	statistician

Quick Quiz B

Directions: Find the misspelled word in each group. Then spell the word correctly on the lines provided for you.

_____	**1.**	pediatrician	electriction
_____	**2.**	burglar	mountian
_____	**3.**	captin	Britain
_____	**4.**	musician	curtin
_____	**5.**	certain	porcelin
_____	**6.**	celler	villain
_____	**7.**	liar	calender
_____	**8.**	statistician	politition
_____	**9.**	burser	cellar
_____	**10.**	curtain	certian

Confusing Vowel Sounds

Some words contain a vowel that has a different sound from its spelling. The following words are hard to spell because of a confusing vowel sound:

Word	Confusing vowel	We say . . .	Not . . .
dollar	a	doll *er*	doll *ar*
benefit	e	ben *uh* fit	ben *ee* fit
despair	e	*dis* pare	*des* pare
existence	e	*ig* zis tense	*egg* zis tense
privilege	i	priv *uh* lij	priv *ih* lij
sponsor	o	spon *sir*	spon *sore*

Many people find words with a confusing vowel the hardest words to spell. As a result, these words are often misspelled. Below are some hints for learning how to spell these words:

1. **Learn** the most commonly misspelled oddball words.

2. **Pronounce** the confusing vowel in an exaggerated way until you have learned the spelling.

3. **Write** the word several times until you know the spelling.

4. **Think** of a related word.

Let's look at the last hint more closely.

You can often figure out the correct vowel in an oddball word by thinking of another word that is a closely related word in which the vowel is said the way it is spelled. Here are some examples:

Vowel	Unclear	Clear
a	narrative	narrate
a	sedative	sedate
e	arithmetic	arithmetical
e	celebrate	celebrity
e	competition	compete
i	hypocrisy	hypocritical
o	revolution	revolt

Quick Quiz C

Directions: Match each misspelled word to its correct spelling. Write the letter of the correct spelling on the lines provided for you:

Misspelled Words	*Words Spelled Correctly*
_____ **1.** privilige	**a.** benefit
_____ **2.** doller	**b.** baker
_____ **3.** defenite	**c.** privilege
_____ **4.** despare	**d.** hypocrisy
_____ **5.** benafit	**e.** despair
_____ **6.** sponser	**f.** sponsor
_____ **7.** arithmitic	**g.** dollar
_____ **8.** celabrate	**h.** arithmetic
_____ **9.** hypocresy	**i.** definite
_____ **10.** bakur	**j.** celebrate

Quick Quiz D

Directions: Below is a list of misspelled words. Each is an oddball word. Correct the spelling of each word and explain why the word is hard to spell. Use the words in the box as your guide.

analyze	dollar	syllable	existence
origin	despair	hypocrisy	terror

Word	Why the Word Is Hard to Spell

1. sillable_____

_____

2. dispair_____

_____

3. terrer_____

_____

4. existance_____

_____

5. analize_____

_____

6. dollr_____

_____

7. orgin_____

_____

8. hypocrisy_____

_____

Some Important Oddball Words

The words listed below don't fit into any clear-cut categories. However, you are likely to use them in your everyday writing and work writing.

biscuit	forfeit
Wednesday	lieutenant
bureau	pigeon
colonel	sergeant
Connecticut	surgeon

Quick Quiz E

Directions: Circle the oddball letter or letters in each of these words. Or, circle the part or parts of each word you find most confusing. Then write each word twice on the lines provided.

1. Wednesday _____ _____

2. bureau _____ _____

3. sergeant _____ _____

4. pigeon _____ _____

5. lieutenant _____ _____

6. colonel _____ _____

7. Connecticut _____ _____

8. forfeit _____ _____

9. surgeon _____ _____

10. biscuit _____ _____

Answers to Quick Quizzes

Answers to Quick Quiz A

1. sympathy
2. cynical
3. paralysis
4. hypocrisy
5. analyze
6. syllable
7. symphony
8. synonym
9. cylinder
10. anonymous

Answers to Quick Quiz B

1. electrician
2. mountain
3. captain
4. curtain
5. porcelain
6. cellar
7. calendar
8. politician
9. bursar
10. certain

Answers to Quick Quiz C

1. c
2. g
3. i
4. e
5. a
6. f
7. h
8. j
9. d
10. b

Answers to Quick Quiz D

Word	Why the Word Is Hard to Spell
1. syllable	*y* creates the *i* sound
2. despair	confusing vowel
3. terror	confusing vowel
4. existence	confusing vowel
5. analyze	*y* creates the *i* sound
6. dollar	confusing vowel
7. origin	confusing vowel
8. hypocrisy	*y* creates the *i* sound

Answers to Quick Quiz E

Answers will vary.

Practice Test

Directions: Choose the word that is not spelled correctly. Spell it correctly on the lines provided for you.

_____ **1.** begger   burglar

_____ **2.** celler   liar

_____ **3.** terror   calender

_____ **4.** Britain   captin

_____ **5.** syllable   simpathy

_____ **6.** hypocrisy   simphony

_____ **7.** bakur   syllable

_____ **8.** villin   ago

_____ **9.** terror   certin

_____ **10.** mountin   curtain

_____ **11.** electric   doller

_____ **12.** musik   benefit

_____ **13.** politic   celabrate

_____ **14.** sponser   revolt

_____ **15.** pediatric   terrur

_____ **16.** forfet   certain

_____ **17.** surgeon   pigun

_____ **18.** sergent   chief

_____ **19.** bureau   liur

_____ **20.** colonel   Wedesday

Answers

1. beggar
2. cellar
3. calendar
4. captain
5. sympathy
6. symphony
7. baker
8. villain
9. certain
10. mountain
11. dollar
12. music
13. celebrate
14. sponsor
15. terror
16. forfeit
17. pigeon
18. sergeant
19. liar
20. Wednesday

Spelling Rules

Contractions and Possessive Nouns | 5

In previous chapters, you learned some of the rules of spelling. For example, you learned the relationship between sounds and letters. In this chapter, you will discover how to spell two other types of words: *contractions* and *possessives*.

What Are *Contractions*?

A *contraction* is a shortened form of two words. Here are three examples:

Contraction	Original Words
I'm	I am
haven't	have not
can't	can not

When you form a contraction, you combine two words and insert an apostrophe (') in the space where the letter or letters have been left out. The process looks like this:

Two Words	Letter(s) Omitted	Contraction
I am	a	I'm
have not	o	haven't
can not	no	can't

Quick Quiz A

Directions: Circle the contractions in each row.

1.	has	hearts	hasn't
2.	its	it's	yours
3.	lets	ours	let's
4.	your	has	you've
5.	I'm	ices	theirs
6.	you're	tickets	yours
7.	cant	covers	can't
8.	houses	haven't	wheels
9.	didn't	digs	dogs
10.	he's	his	shoes

How to Spell Contractions

The following chart shows how to spell the most common contractions. Study the chart carefully because some of these words may look unfamiliar to you. For example, the words *will + not* combine to form the contraction *won't,* not *willn't.*

Word #1		Word #2		Contraction
does	+	not	=	doesn't
can	+	not	=	can't
could	+	not	=	couldn't
has	+	not	=	hasn't
he	+	is	=	he's
he	+	will	=	he'll
I	+	am	=	I'm
I	+	have	=	I've
it	+	is	=	it's
it	+	will	=	it'll
let	+	us	=	let's
must	+	not	=	mustn't
she	+	would	=	she'd
she	+	will	=	she'll
there	+	is	=	there's
they	+	are	=	they're
they	+	will	=	they'll
was	+	not	=	wasn't
we	+	are	=	we're
we	+	have	=	we've
we	+	would	=	we'd
we	+	will	=	we'll
were	+	not	=	weren't
who	+	is	=	who's
will	+	not	=	won't
would	+	not	=	wouldn't
you	+	are	=	you're
you	+	have	=	you've

Quick Quiz B

Directions: Make each of the underlined pairs of words into a contraction. Write your answers on the lines provided for you.

1. If you <u>do not</u> know how to study, try different methods until you find the one that works best for you.

   _____

2. People who live in glass houses are the ones who <u>should not</u> throw stones.

   _____

3. If it <u>was not</u> for our own determination, we <u>would not</u> be able to achieve our goals.

   _____

4. <u>Do not</u> be irreplaceable: If you <u>can not</u> be replaced, you <u>can not</u> be promoted.

   _____

5. It <u>does not</u> matter what you say: It only matters what <u>you have</u> done and what <u>you are</u> going to do.

   _____

6. <u>It is</u> important to learn how to spell correctly.

   _____

7. Even if <u>you have</u> been fishing for 3 hours and you <u>have not</u> gotten anything except poison ivy and sunburn, <u>you are</u> still better off than the worm.

   _____

8. <u>I am</u> sure that earning a GED is one of the best things a person can do for his or her future.

   _____

9. The light bulbs in the New York subway system screw in clockwise and screw out counterclockwise, the reverse of traditional light bulbs. This is so that people who steal them <u>can not</u> use them.

   _____

10. <u>It is not</u> difficult to learn new skills, if you break them into smaller tasks.

   _____

Quick Quiz C

Directions: Make each of the contractions into the two words that it re-placed. Write your answer on the lines provided for you.

Here's an example:

<u>It's</u> important to save for the future.

Answer: <u>It is</u>

1. If you <u>can't</u> understand an important concept, you <u>mustn't</u> get discouraged. Stick with it and <u>you'll</u> catch on.

_____

2. The IRS: <u>We've</u> got what it takes to get what <u>you've</u> got.

_____

3. <u>I've</u> learned that a little hard work goes a long way toward success.

_____

4. My doctor said, "<u>You're</u> sick—but <u>it's</u> going to get better soon."

_____

5. <u>Don't</u> get discouraged by the amount of work you have to do.

_____

6. I <u>couldn't</u> study on Tuesday, but it <u>didn't</u> matter because <u>I'll</u> make it up on Wednesday.

_____

Contractions and Possessive Pronouns

Contractions and possessive pronouns may look the same, but they are not. Here's a chart to help you compare the two different parts of speech:

Contraction	Possessive Pronoun
it's (it is)	its
you're (you are)	your
they're (they are)	their
who's (who is)	whose

What Is *Possession?*

Possession shows ownership. Below are two ways to show possession:

The pen that belongs to Maria.   Maria's pen.

While both ways of showing possession are correct, we usually use the second way—"Maria's pen"—because it is less wordy.

In many languages other than English, the object that is possessed is named first, followed by the person or thing that possesses it.

For example: *This is the office of Spencer.*

As a result, the way possessives are formed in English often poses problems for non-native speakers. Therefore, if English is not your first language, pay special attention to this chapter.

How to Form Possessive Nouns

Follow these simple rules to spell possessive nouns correctly:

1. With singular nouns, add an apostrophe and an *s*:

Not possessive	*Possessive*
child	child's toy
lion	lion's roar
Charles	Charles's job

   Note: Often, people drop the *s* after the apostrophe in a singular possessive noun that ends in *s*. This is perfectly acceptable:

Acceptable	*Also acceptable*
James's book	James' book
Rozakis's advice	Rozakis' advice

2. With plural nouns ending in *s*, add an apostrophe after the *s*:

Not possessive	*Possessive*
clients	clients' receipts
workers	workers' ideas
explorers	explorers' parkas

3. With plural nouns not ending in *s*, add an apostrophe and an *s*:

Not possessive	*Possessive*
fish	fish's tails
women	women's trucks
men	men's cars
mice	mice's tails

4. To form the possessive of a business name, joint owner, or compound noun, just put an apostrophe and *s* after the **last** word:

Not possessive	*Possessive*
Bikel and Bikel	Bikel and Bikel's cases
Gilbert and Sullivan	Gilbert and Sullivan's operas
sister-in-law	sister-in-law's bracelet

Quick Quiz D

Directions: Underline the correct possessive form for each phrase. The first one is done for you.

1. the suggestion of James

   Jame's suggestion   <u>James's suggestion</u>

2. the role of the lifeguard

   lifeguard's role   lifeguards' role

3. the colors of the clouds

   clouds' colors   cloud's colors

4. the anger of the boss

   bos's anger   boss's anger

5. the book of Dickens

   Dickens' book   Dicken's book

6. the sand of the beaches

   beache's sand   beaches' sand

7. the votes of the people

   people's votes   peop'les votes

8. the pledge of the Girl Scouts

   Girl Scout's pledge   Girl Scouts' pledge

9. the pencil of the editor-in-chief

   editor-in-chief's pencil   editor's-in-chiefs pencil

10. the strokes of the swimmers

    swimmers' strokes   swimmer's strokes

Quick Quiz E

Directions: In this exercise, use the possessive form to shorten each of the following sentences. Write your answer on the lines provided for you.

Here is an example:

Original:

The car horns of most Americans beep in the key of "F."

Revised:

Most Americans' car horns beep in the key of "F."

1. The eye of an ostrich is bigger than its brain.

_____

_____

2. The temperature in eastern Siberia can get so cold that the moisture in the breath of a person can freeze in the air and fall to the ground.

_____

_____

3. Lincoln Logs were invented by the son of Frank Lloyd Wright.

_____

_____

4. The original name of Mickey Mouse was "Mortimer Mouse."

_____

_____

5. The real name of Hulk Hogan is "Terry Bollea."

_____

_____

6. The milk of a camel does not curdle.

_____

_____

7. In "Fantasia" by Disney, the name of the Sorcerer is "Yensid," which is "Disney" spelled backward.

_____

_____

8. The height of the Eiffel Tower varies by as much as 6 inches, depending on the temperature.

_____

_____

9. The favorite hobby of my mother-in-law is gambling at the slot machines.

_____

_____

10. The hearts of women beat faster than the hearts of men.

_____

_____

Answers to Quick Quizzes

Answers to Quick Quiz A

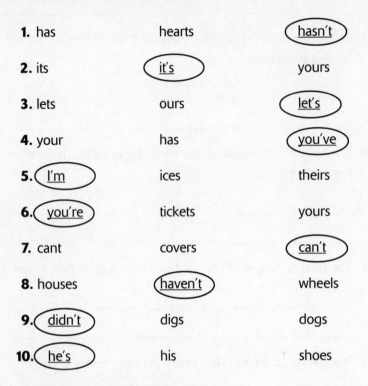

1. has	hearts	(hasn't)
2. its	(it's)	yours
3. lets	ours	(let's)
4. your	has	(you've)
5. (I'm)	ices	theirs
6. (you're)	tickets	yours
7. cant	covers	(can't)
8. houses	(haven't)	wheels
9. (didn't)	digs	dogs
10. (he's)	his	shoes

Answers to Quick Quiz B

1. don't

2. shouldn't

3. wasn't, wouldn't

4. Don't, can't, can't

5. doesn't, you've, you're

6. It's

7. you've, haven't, you're

8. I'm

9. can't

10. Isn't

Answers to Quick Quiz C

1. can not, must not, you will

2. We have, you have

3. I have

4. You are, it is

5. Do not

6. could not, did not, I will

Answers to Quick Quiz D

2. lifeguard's role

3. clouds' colors

4. boss's anger

5. Dickens' book

6. beaches' sand

7. people's votes

8. Girl Scouts' pledge

9. editor-in-chief's pencil

10. swimmers' strokes

Answers to Quick Quiz E

1. An ostrich's eye is bigger than its brain.

2. The temperature in eastern Siberia can get so cold that the moisture in a person's breath can freeze in the air and fall to the ground.

3. Lincoln Logs were invented by Frank Lloyd Wright's son.

4. Mickey Mouse's original name was "Mortimer Mouse."

5. Hulk Hogan's real name is "Terry Bollea."

6. Camel's milk does not curdle.

7. In Disney's "Fantasia," the Sorcerer's name is "Yensid," which is "Disney" spelled backward.

8. The Eiffel Tower's height varies by as much as 6 inches, depending on the temperature.

9. My mother-in-law's favorite hobby is gambling at the slot machines.

10. Women's hearts beat faster than men's hearts.

Practice Test

Directions: Some of the following words are misspelled. Write **C** if the word is spelled correctly and write **X** if it is spelled incorrectly. Then write the words correctly on the lines provided for you.

_____**1.** can't   _____**6.** Phyllis' hair

_____**2.** does'nt   _____**7.** ladie's desserts

_____**3.** he'll   _____**8.** citie's problems

_____**4.** they're   _____**9.** father-in-law's fishing

_____**5.** couldnt   _____**10.** Jill's books

Write the misspelled words correctly:

_____   _____

_____   _____

Answers

C	**1.** can't	C	**6.** Phyllis' hair
X	**2.** does'nt	X	**7.** ladie's desserts
C	**3.** he'll	X	**8.** citie's problems
C	**4.** they're	C	**9.** father-in-law's fishing
X	**5.** couldn't	C	**10.** Jill's books

Misspelled Words Corrected

2. doesn't

5. couldn't

7. ladies'

8. cities'

Plural Nouns | 6

In this chapter, we're going to teach you how to take *singular* nouns and change them into *plural* nouns.

What Are *Singular* and *Plural Nouns*?

- *Singular* means "one person, place, or thing."
- *Plural* means "more than one person, place, or thing."

Here are some examples:

Singular Noun	Plural Noun
hand (one hand)	hands (more than one hand)
tree (one tree)	trees (more than one tree)
child (one child)	children (more than one child)

Some nouns form *regular plurals*. This means that you can just add an -*s* or -*es* to them to make them plural. Other nouns, however, do not follow these rules. These are called *irregular plurals*. Here are some examples:

Regular Plurals	
Singular Noun	**Plural Noun**
car	cars
box	boxes
nose	noses

Irregular Plurals	
Singular Noun	Plural Noun
foot	feet
louse	lice
man	men

The regular plurals are easy to form, but it is those irregular plurals that often cause spelling trouble. If you can remember some simple rules, you will be able to spell these words correctly.

How to Form the Plural of Regular Nouns

Follow these guidelines to form the plural of regular nouns:

- Most regular plurals are formed by adding *s* to the end of the word:

Singular	*Plural*
arrow	arrows
bird	birds
dog	dogs
duck	ducks
hat	hats
pencil	pencils

- Add *es* if the noun ends in *s*, *sh*, *ch*, or *x*:

Singular	*Plural*
class	classes
inch	inches
Jones	Joneses
roach	roaches
sex	sexes
stress	stresses
tax	taxes

Quick Quiz A

Directions: Underline the plural word that is spelled correctly in each line.

1. sparrows   hatsz   bushs

2. boxes   friendss   churchs

3. circuss   views   boxs

4. newspaperz   peaches   dishs

5. taxes   nosez   foxs

- If a consonant comes before the letter *y*, change the *y* to *i* and add *es*:

Singular	*Plural*
activity	activities
blueberry	blueberries
city	cities
cry	cries
lady	ladies

- But if the noun ends in *y* and a <u>vowel</u> comes before the *y*, add *s*:

Singular	*Plural*
attorney	attorneys
boy	boys
essay	essays
honey	honeys
journey	journeys
monkey	monkeys
ray	rays
survey	surveys

Note: Words that end in -*quy*, as in *soliloquy—soliloquies* do not follow this rule.

Quick Quiz B

Directions: Each of the following words is spelled incorrectly. Write the correct spelling on the lines provided for you.

1. enemys _____

2. holidaies _____

3. mysterys _____

4. turkies _____

5. tragedys _____

6. memorys _____

- If the noun ends in *o* and a <u>vowel</u> comes before that *o*, add *s*:

Singular	*Plural*
cameo	cameos
folio	folios
patio	patios
radio	radios
ratio	ratios
studio	studios

Quick Quiz C

Directions: Complete the following exercise by writing the plural form of each word on the lines provided for you.

Singular	*Plural*
1. lily	_____
2. rodeo	_____
3. tattoo	_____
4. alto	_____
5. studio	_____

- If the noun ends in *o*, and a <u>consonant</u> comes before the *o*, you can add *es* or *s*:

Singular	*Plural*
takes *es*	
echo	echoes
hero	heroes
potato	potatoes
tomato	tomatoes

Singular	*Plural*
takes *s*	
alto	altos
dynamo	dynamos
piano	pianos
silo	silos
solo	solos
soprano	sopranos

Singular	*Plural*
takes either *es* or *s*	
buffalo	buffalos, buffaloes
cargo	cargos, cargoes
domino	dominos, dominoes
motto	mottos, mottoes
tornado	tornados, tornadoes
zero	zeros, zeroes

- Add *s* to most nouns that end with the letter *f*:

Singular	*Plural*
belief	beliefs
brief	briefs
chief	chiefs
proof	proofs
staff	staffs

There are, of course, exceptions to this rule. In some cases, you'll need to change the *f* or *fe* to *v* and add *es*:

Singular	*Plural*
half	halves
knife	knives
leaf	leaves
life	lives
self	selves
thief	thieves
wife	wives
wolf	wolves

However, for people's names, just add an *s*: Mr. and Ms. *Wolf* becomes the *Wolfs*.

- Words that end in *-ey*, *-ay*, or *-oy* do not have *-ies* plurals:

Singular   *Plural*

-ey

abbey   abbeys

jitney   jitneys

valley   valleys

-ay

clay   clays

tray   trays

play   plays

-oy

ploy   ploys

toy   toys

boy   boys

- In compound words, make the <u>main word</u> plural:

Singular   *Plural*

mother-in-law   mothers-in-law

passerby   passersby

sister-in-law   sisters-in-law

However, there are two exceptions. Here's the first: If there is no noun in the compound word, add an *s* to the end of the word:

Singular   *Plural*

mix-up   mix-ups

takeoff   takeoffs

Here's the second: If the compound word ends in *-ful*, add an *s* to the end of the word:

Singular   *Plural*

cupful   cupfuls

mouthful   mouthfuls

Quick Quiz D

Directions: Some of the following words are misspelled. Write **C** if the word is spelled correctly and write **X** if it is spelled incorrectly. Then write the misspelled words correctly on the lines provided for you.

_____**1.** vetos   _____**6.** selves

_____**2.** pianos   _____**7.** wifes

_____**3.** tomatos   _____**8.** knives

_____**4.** proofs   _____**9.** vallies

_____**5.** sheriffes   _____**10.** sisters-ins-laws

Write the misspelled words correctly:

_____   _____

_____   _____

_____   _____

How to Form the Plural of Irregular Nouns

When you form the plural of *irregular* nouns, follow these guidelines:

- Some nouns change their spelling when they become plural. For example:

Singular	*Plural*
child	children
foot	feet
goose	geese
louse	lice
man	men
mouse	mice
ox	oxen
tooth	teeth
woman	women

- But, some nouns stay the same whether they are singular or plural. Here are some examples:

Singular	*Plural*
deer	deer
moose	moose
Portuguese	Portuguese
series	series
sheep	sheep
species	species
swine	swine

- Foreign words can have unusual plural forms. Here are some examples:

Singular	Plural
alumnus	alumni (female)
alumna	alumnae (male)
analysis	analyses
axis	axes
bacterium	bacteria
basis	bases
crisis	crises
criterion	criteria
hypothesis	hypotheses
index	index, indices
memorandum	memorandums, memoranda
parenthesis	parentheses
phenomenon	phenomena
stimulus	stimuli
thesis	theses

Quick Quiz E

Directions: Write the plural form of each of the following words on the lines provided for you.

Singular   Plural

1. man   _____

2. goose   _____

3. deer   _____

4. species   _____

5. Vietnamese   _____

6. Lebanese   _____

7. parenthesis   _____

8. memorandum   _____or_____

9. bacterium   _____

10. criterion   _____

Answers to Quick Quizzes

Answers to Quick Quiz A

1. sparrows

2. boxes

3. views

4. peaches

5. taxes

Answers to Quick Quiz B

1. enemies

2. holidays

3. mysteries

4. turkeys

5. tragedies

6. memories

Answers to Quick Quiz C

1. lilies

2. rodeos

3. tattoos

4. altos

5. studios

Answers to Quick Quiz D

_X_	**1.** vetos	_C_	**6.** selves
_C_	**2.** pianos	_X_	**7.** wifes
_X_	**3.** tomatos	_C_	**8.** knives
_C_	**4.** proofs	_X_	**9.** vallies
_X_	**5.** sheriffes	_X_	**10.** sisters-ins-laws

Misspelled Words Corrected

1. vetoes

3. tomatoes

5. sheriffs

7. wives

9. valleys

10. sisters-in-law

Answers to Quick Quiz E

1. men

2. geese

3. deer

4. species

5. Vietnamese

6. Lebanese

7. parentheses

8. memorandums *or* memoranda

9. bacteria

10. criteria

Practice Test

Directions: Choose the word that is not spelled correctly. Spell it correctly on the lines provided for you.

_____**1.** newspapers   happiness   raspberrys

_____**2.** gloves   iciness   childs

_____**3.** magazines   birdes   countries

_____**4.** inches   activitys   arrows

_____**5.** heros   classes   sopranos

_____**6.** sexes   tomatos   essays

_____**7.** potatos   pigeons   taxes

_____**8.** halfs   journeys   beliefs

_____**9.** cameos   radios   wifes

_____**10.** monkeys   echoes   bacterias

Answers

1. raspberries
2. children
3. birds
4. activities
5. heroes
6. tomatoes
7. potatoes
8. halves
9. wives
10. bacteria

Helpful Spelling Rules 7

When people first started writing English, there weren't many rules. Since so few people could write, there was no one to say what was spelled correctly and what wasn't. People even spelled their own names different ways! For instance, William Shakespeare spelled his name one way on his plays and he spelled it another way on his last will and testament. Someone else spelled it still another way on his tombstone!

In 1775, Samuel Johnson published his *Dictionary of the English Language.* By then, spelling had become fairly standardized but, even so, Johnson's dictionary was important because it gave people a way to check their spelling. With everyone using the same spelling, there was a greater chance that people could be understood and there was less chance of misreadings and mistakes. Johnson based his spelling rules on the history of each word.

In 1828, Noah Webster published his *American Dictionary of the English Language* and his *American Spelling Book.* Both books became very famous because they were very useful. As a matter of fact, Webster's *American Spelling Book* sold more than sixty million copies!

By this time, people understood how much spelling mattered. It had become one of the signs of an educated, intelligent person. In this chapter and the next one, we'll teach you some important spelling rules. Learning just a handful of spelling rules can help you spell many, many words correctly and this will help you get your meaning across in writing. As a result, you will earn a higher score on both the Language Arts, Writing and the Language Arts, Reading tests of the GED. In addition, you will feel more confident when you write.

Rule #1: *i* before *e* except after *c* . . .

This is one of the most useful spelling rules. It has a catchy rhythm that makes it easy to remember. Perhaps you have heard it before:

i before *e* except after *c*

or as sounded as *a* as in *neighbor* and *weigh*

Here are some words that fit the rule:

i before *e*   except after *c* sounded as *a*

achieve	ceiling	beige
believe	conceit	eight
bier	conceive	feint
chief	deceit	freight
fiend	deceive	heir
friend	perceive	neighbor
fierce	receipt	reign
grief	receive	sleigh
piece	surveillance	
relief	veil	
relieve	vein	
shriek	weigh	
siege	weight	
yield		

Here are some words that do *not* fit the rule:

codeine	counterfeit
either	Fahrenheit
feirie	financier
foreign	glacier
height	neither
leisure	protein
seize	weird

Follow these suggestions to make it easier for you to tell when to use *ie* and when to use *ei*:

- In most cases, when the *c* sounds like *sh*, the order of the letters is *ie*, not *ei*. Words that fit this rule include the following:

ancient

coefficient

conscientious

efficient

prescience

- Words with *i* and *e* pronounced with a long *a* sound are always spelled *-ei*, never *-ie*. Here are some examples:

  eight

  feign

  neigh

  peignoir (nightgown)

  sleigh

  vein

- If the sound is a long *i*, the word is usually spelled with the *-ei* combo, not *-ie*. For example:

  feisty

  height

  stein

  seismic

  Here are the common exceptions: *hierarchy, fiery,* and *hieroglyphic. Notice that in each case, the* "-ie" *combination is followed by an* r.

- *ie* words with a short vowel sound are usually spelled *-ie* rather than *-ei*. Here are some examples:

  friend

  handkerchief

  mischief

  patient

  sieve

  transient

  Here are some words that do NOT fit this rule:

  counterfeit

  heifer

  nonpareil

  sovereign

  surfeit

- Last, think of *ie* and *ei* words that give you special trouble. Perhaps it's *financier,* maybe *foreign.* Make a special effort to memorize these words. Use the rhyming rule to help you remember them.

Quick Quiz A

Directions: Write the *ie/ei* word that matches each clue. Use the words from the word box as your guide.

fiend	chief
beige	yield
deceive	piece
eight	vein
weight	grief

1. artery _____

2. give up _____

3. section, part _____

4. deep sadness _____

5. trick _____

6. main _____

7. bad guy _____

8. one more than seven _____

9. tan color _____

10. heaviness, importance _____

Quick Quiz B

Directions: Complete the following words by adding *-ie* or *-ei* as necessary.

1. w____rd

2. ____ght

3. s____ze

4. caff____ne

5. forf____t

6. dec____ve

7. s____ve

8. h____ght

9. c____ling

10. fr____nd

11. rec____pt

12. conc____ve

13. p____ce

14. w____ld

15. n____ce

Rule #2: The *-ceed/-cede* rule

There are only three verbs in English that end in *-ceed*: *succeed*, *proceed*, and *exceed*. All the other verbs with that sound end in *-cede*. For example:

accede   cede
concede   intercede
precede   recede
secede

There is only one English verb that ends in *-sede*: *supersede*.

Quick Quiz C

Directions: Each of the following words is misspelled. Spell it correctly on the lines provided for you.

1. receede _____

2. preceede _____

3. consede _____

4. intersede _____

5. acceede _____

6. supercede _____

Rule #3: The *-ful* rule

Remember that the sound *full* at the end of a word is spelled with only one *l*. For example:

Root Word +	Suffix	=	New Word
care	+	ful	=	careful
grace	+	ful	=	graceful
health	+	ful	=	healthful
hope	+	ful	=	hopeful

When the suffix is *-ful* plus *-ly,* the word has two *l*'s. Here are some examples:

Root Word +	Suffix	=	New Word
restful	+	ly	=	restfully
baleful	+	ly	=	balefully
thankful	+	ly	=	thankfully
mirthful	+	ly	=	mirthfully
artful	+	ly	=	artfully
zestful	+	ly	=	zestfully

Quick Quiz D

Directions: Underline the misspelled word in each line. Then spell the word correctly on the lines provided for you.

1. trustfull   sinful   fretful   _____

2. flavorful   healthfull   harmful   _____

3. carefull   hurtful   tasteful   _____

4. wonderful   tasteful   beautifull   _____

5. trustful   joyful   painfuly   _____

6. restfully   colorfuly   hurtfully   _____

7. thankfuly   zestfully   artfully   _____

8. awfully   hopefuly   mirthfully   _____

Rule #4: -ery or -ary?

Knowing when to use *-ery* or *-ary* at the end of a word can be confusing. Fortunately, there is a spelling rule to cover this spelling problem.

First, only six everyday words end with *-ery* as opposed to *-ary*. The words are:

cemetery
confectionery
distillery
millinery
monastery
stationery

Therefore, if you have to guess, go with *-ary* rather than *-ery*.

Quick Quiz E

Directions: Spell each of the following words correctly. Then write the rule that you used on the lines provided for you.

Spelling Word   Rule

1. superseed _____

_____

2. healthfull _____

_____

3. exced _____

_____

4. stationery _____

_____

5. balefuly _____

_____

6. confectionary _____

_____

7. intersede _____

_____

8. mirthfuly _____

_____

9. monastary _____

_____

10. presede _____

_____

Answers to Quick Quizzes

Answers to Quick Quiz A

1. vein
2. yield
3. piece
4. grief
5. deceive
6. chief
7. fiend
8. eight
9. beige
10. weight

Answers to Quick Quiz B

1. weird
2. eight
3. seize
4. caffeine
5. forfeit
6. deceive
7. sieve
8. height
9. ceiling
10. friend
11. receipt
12. conceive
13. piece
14. wield
15. niece

Answers to Quick Quiz C

1. recede
2. precede
3. concede
4. intercede
5. accede
6. supersede

Answers to Quick Quiz D

1. trustful
2. healthful
3. careful
4. beautiful
5. painfully
6. colorfully
7. thankfully
8. hopefully

Answers to Quick Quiz E

Spelling Word	Rule
1. supersede	This is the only English verb that ends in *-sede*.
2. healthful	The sound *full* at the end of a word is spelled with only one *l*.
3. exceed	There are only three verbs in English that end in *-ceed* and this is one of them.
4. stationary	Only six everyday words end with *-ery* as opposed to *-ary* and this is NOT one of them.
5. balefully	When the suffix is *-ful* plus *-ly,* there are two *l*'s.
6. confectionery	Only six everyday words end with *-ery* as opposed to *-ary,* and *this* is one of them.
7. intercede	The verb with the "ceed" sound ends in *-cede*.
8. mirthfully	When the suffix is *-ful* plus *-ly,* the word has two *l*'s.
9. monastery	This is one of only six everyday words that ends with *-ery* rather than *-ary*.
10. precede	The verb with the "ceed" sound ends in *-cede*.

Practice Test

Directions: Some of the following words are misspelled. Write **C** if the word is spelled correctly and write **X** if the word is spelled incorrectly. Then write the misspelled words correctly on the lines provided for you.

_____**1.** beleive

_____**2.** achieve

_____**3.** careful

_____**4.** conceit

_____**5.** hopefull

_____**6.** cieling

_____**7.** intercede

_____**8.** either

_____**9.** helpfull

_____**10.** Fahrenhiet

_____**11.** restfully

_____**12.** precede

_____**13.** weigh

_____**14.** nieghbor

_____**15.** cemetery

Write the misspelled words correctly:

_____   _____

_____   _____

_____   _____

Answers

  X   **1.** beleive

  C   **2.** achieve

  C   **3.** careful

  C   **4.** conceit

  X   **5.** hopefull

  X   **6.** cieling

  C   **7.** intercede

  C   **8.** either

  X   **9.** helpfull

  X **10.** Fahrenhiet

  C **11.** restfully

  C **12.** precede

  C **13.** weigh

  X **14.** nieghbor

  C **15.** cemetery

Misspelled Words Corrected

1. believe

5. hopeful

6. ceiling

9. helpful

10. Fahrenheit

14. neighbor

More Helpful Spelling Rules | 8

In this chapter, we'll explain three more spelling rules. Learning these rules is a shortcut to becoming a good speller. That's because learning just one rule can help you spell many, many words correctly. Learning a handful of spelling rules gives you a wealth of words that you will be able to use with confidence in your writing.

Rule #5: *q* is followed by *u*

In just about every English word that has a *q*, the *q* is directly followed by a *u*. Therefore, the pattern is *qu*. Here are some examples:

quack	quad	quadrant
quadrennial	quadrilateral	quadriceps
quadrille	quadruped	quadruple
quadruplet	quaff	quail
quake	qualification	qualify
qualm	quantity	quarantine
quark	quarrel	quarry
quart	quarter	quartz
quay	queasy	queen
queer	quench	quest
question	quick	quicken
quickly	quicksand	quiet
quill	quilt	quince
quintet	quit	quite
quiver	quiz	quotation

The exceptions are "made-up" words such *qiana* (a lightweight nylon fabric) or words that we use in English, but come from foreign languages. An example is *Qatar*, the east Arabian Peninsula on the Persian Gulf. The word *Qatar* can also be spelled "Katar."

The rule doesn't fit with abbreviations, however. For instance, the abbreviation for *quart* is *qt.* (not *qut.*)

Quick Quiz A

Directions: Underline the misspelled word in each line. Then write the word correctly on the lines provided for you.

_____	**1.** qualification	qarrel	quarter
_____	**2.** queen	qite	quail
_____	**3.** qualm	quiet	qilt
_____	**4.** quadrant	quart	qickly
_____	**5.** qauke	quarantine	quick
_____	**6.** quad	quantity	qeustion
_____	**7.** quadruped	qeust	quicksand
_____	**8.** quack	qartz	quiver
_____	**9.** qualify	quarry	qiut
_____	**10.** qiz	quotation	quotable

Quick Quiz B

Directions: Each of the following words is misspelled. Spell it correctly on the lines provided for you.

1. qaint

_____

2. qalification

_____

3. eqality

_____

4. qotient

_____

5. iniuqity

_____

6. qota

_____

7. qiubble

_____

8. qeunch

_____

9. qestion

_____

10. qiuckly

_____

Rule #6: *k*'s and *c*'s

Some words that end in *c* have a hard *k* sound. Adding *y*, *i*, or *e* after the final *c* changes the hard sound to a soft one, creating spelling problems. Here's the rule:

Add a *k* after the final *c* when the hard sound becomes soft.

Here are some examples:

Word ending in c	*Adding the* k
picnic	picnicked, picnicking, picnicker
mimic	mimicked, mimicking, mimicker
politic	politicking
traffic	trafficked, trafficking, trafficker
panic	panicked, panicking, panicky

Quick Quiz C

Directions: Using the rules you've learned so far in this chapter, spell each of the following words correctly. Write the rule next to each spelling word on the lines provided for you.

Word	Correct Spelling	Rule
1. qiute	_____	_____
2. mimiced	_____	_____
3. euqal	_____	_____
4. picniced	_____	_____
5. qaurt	_____	_____
6. panicing	_____	_____
7. qota	_____	_____
8. trafficer	_____	_____
9. qiuck	_____	_____
10. politicing	_____	_____

Rule #7: Spelling Hyphenated Words

Spelling involves not only letters but also spaces. It also involves symbols. Among the most important are *hyphens*. Do not confuse a hyphen and a dash.

A *hyphen* and a *dash* are two completely different marks of punctuation. Notice that a dash is twice as long as a hyphen.

This is a *hyphen*: -

This is a *dash*: —

A dash and a hyphen have completely different uses in writing.

- A *dash* means that there is a sharp change of thought. A dash is used between parts of sentences.

  For example: The GED is an important test—it can help you in many ways.

- A *hyphen* is used within parts of words.

  For example: mother-in-law   ninety-nine   pro-American

  A hyphen is most often used to create compound words.

Compound words fall into three categories:

- hyphenated compounds
- open compounds
- closed compounds

Let's look at hyphenated compounds first.
Hyphenated compounds are joined with a hyphen: Here are some examples:

comparison-contrast   old-fashioned

nurse-practitioner   bell-like

secretary-treasurer   able-bodied

Some words begin their life without a hyphen, adopt one, and then drop it. *Steamboat*, for example, was once *steam boat*, then *steam-boat*. Today, we spell it without a hyphen as *steamboat*.

Quick Quiz D

Directions: Add one or more hyphens to each word, as required. Then rewrite the hyphenated word on the lines provided for you.

1. greatgrandfather _____

2. fiveyearolds   _____

3. sisterinlaw   _____

4. wellorganized   _____

5. afterschool   _____

6. wellattended   _____

7. allaround   _____

8. selfeducated   _____

9. farfetched   _____

10. quickwitted   _____

11. soughtafter   _____

12. massproduced   _____

Now, let's look at the other two kinds of compound words, *open compounds* and *closed compounds*:

1. *Open compounds* are written as two words. Here are some examples:

   cedar shingles   bow tie

   night shift   hard work

   executive secretary   student union

2. *Closed compounds* are written as one word. Here are some examples:

   handbook   landowner

   northeast   gallbladder

   homemaker   lawsuit

Quick Quiz E

Directions: Make as many compound words as you can from the following words on the lines provided for you. If you wish, use a dictionary to help you.

1. sun

_____   _____

_____   _____

_____   _____

_____   _____

2. over

_____   _____

_____   _____

_____   _____

3. super

_____   _____

_____   _____

_____   _____

Answer to Quick Quizzes

Answers to Quick Quiz A

1. quarrel
2. quite
3. quilt
4. quickly
5. quake
6. question
7. quest
8. quartz
9. quit
10. quiz

Answers to Quick Quiz B

1. quaint
2. qualification
3. equality
4. quotient
5. iniquity
6. quota
7. quibble
8. quench
9. question
10. quickly

Answers to Quick Quiz C

Correct Spelling	Spelling Rule
1. quite	*q* is followed by *u*
2. mimicked	add a *k* after the final *c* when the hard sound becomes soft
3. equal	*q* is followed by *u*
4. picnicked	add a *k* after the final *c* when the hard sound becomes soft
5. quart	*q* is followed by *u*
6. panicking	add a *k* after the final *c* when the hard sound becomes soft
7. quota	*q* is followed by *u*
8. trafficker	add a *k* after the final *c* when the hard sound becomes soft
9. quick	*q* is followed by *u*
10. politicking	add a *k* after the final *c* when the hard sound becomes soft

Answers to Quick Quiz D

1. great-grandfather
2. five-year-olds
3. sister-in-law
4. well-organized
5. after-school
6. well-attended
7. all-around
8. self-educated
9. far-fetched
10. quick-witted
11. sought-after
12. mass-produced

Possible Answers to Quick Quiz E

sun:

sunbathe	sunbeam
sunburn	Sunday
sundown	sunflower
sunglasses	sunlamp
sunlight	sunrise
sunset	sunshine
sunstroke	sunup

over:

overhear	overhead
overdress	overdone
overcome	overhaul
overpower	overlap

super:

superhuman	superman
supermarket	supernatural
supersonic	superstar
supervision	superstar

Practice Test

Directions: Some of the following words are misspelled. Write **C** if the word is spelled correctly and write **X** if the word is spelled incorrectly. Then write the misspelled words correctly on the lines provided for you.

_____**1.** qake

_____**2.** quarry

_____**3.** qeuen

_____**4.** quite

_____**5.** picnicing

_____**6.** mimicked

_____**7.** night shift

_____**8.** sixty-six

_____**9.** oldfashioned

_____**10.** outlaw

_____**11.** black berry

_____**12.** weekday

_____**13.** ringside

_____**14.** stair-way

_____**15.** eggbeater

Write the misspelled words correctly:

_____   _____

_____   _____

_____   _____

Answers

<u> X </u> **1.** qake

<u> C </u> **2.** quarry

<u> X </u> **3.** qeuen

<u> C </u> **4.** quite

<u> X </u> **5.** picnicing

<u> C </u> **6.** mimicked

<u> C </u> **7.** night shift

<u> C </u> **8.** sixty-six

<u> X </u> **9.** oldfashioned

<u> C </u> **10.** outlaw

<u> X </u> **11.** black berry

<u> C </u> **12.** weekday

<u> C </u> **13.** ringside

<u> X </u> **14.** stair-way

<u> C </u> **15.** eggbeater

Misspelled Words Corrected

1. quake

3. queen

5. picnicking

9. old-fashioned

11. blackberry

14. stairway

Putting the Words Together

Word Roots 9

Many English words are built of three elements: *roots*, *prefixes*, and *suffixes*.

- *Roots*: are the basic building blocks of words.

- *Prefixes*: are added to the <u>front</u> of a word to change its meaning

- *Suffixes*: are added to the <u>end</u> of a word to change its meaning

Here are some examples:

Prefix	+	Root	+	Suffix	=	Word
de		hydrate		ion		dehydration
ab		duct		ed		abducted
in		cred		ible		incredible

If you know how to spell just a handful of roots, prefixes, and suffixes, you will be able to spell many useful words. That is because you will recognize the individual parts and see how they fit together. In this chapter, you will learn how to spell many roots. You will also learn how to spell common words formed from these roots.

What Are Roots?

A *root* is a stem or base form for many words.

1. Some roots form whole words by themselves. For example:

   - *Arbor* means "tree."

   - *Vent* means "opening to allow air to enter."

   - *Omni* means "all."

111

2. Some roots must be combined with other word elements to form words. For example:

Root	Meaning	+	Suffix	=	New Word
capit	head	+	al	=	capital
carn	flesh	+	age	=	carnage
chrono	time	+	logy	=	chronology

3. A word can contain more than one root:

   Matrilineal contains the roots *matra* and *lineal.*

   Matra means "mother."

   Lineal means "line."

4. When it comes to building words from roots, placement matters. Some roots can also function as prefixes, depending on their placement in a word. For example, *graphy* means "writing."

   used as a root   *calligraphy*

   used as a prefix *graphology*

Roots for Measurement

Many of the words we use come from Greek roots.

Below are some important Greek roots for measurements. You will see that some of the roots have more than one spelling. For example, *macro* and *mega* both mean "large."

Root	Meaning	Example	Definition
acr/acro	topmost	acrophobia	fear of high places (*ak* roh foh bee uh)
arch	chief	archbishop	highest bishop
chron	time	chronicle	historical record
ger	old	geriatric	relating to old age (*ger* ee at trik)
horo	hour	horoscope	signs of the zodiac (*hor* oh scope)
macro	large	macroscopic	seen with the naked eye
mega	large	megalith	huge stone
meter	measure	altimeter	device to measure altitude (*al* tih mee ter)
micro	small	microbe	tiny organism (*my* kroh bub)
neo	new	neophyte	beginner (*knee* oh fite)
pan	all	panacea	a cure-all (panay *see* uh)
ped	foot	pedometer	tool for measuring steps (*peh* dom oh ter)
poly	many	polygon	figure with many sides
prot	first	prototype	first of its kind
tele	far off	telescope	device for seeing distant objects

Quick Quiz A

Directions: Match each root to its meaning. Place the letter on the lines provided for you.

_____ **1.** arch   **a.** small

_____ **2.** chron   **b.** large

_____ **3.** horo   **c.** first

_____ **4.** mega   **d.** chief

_____ **5.** meter   **e.** all

_____ **6.** micro   **f.** many

_____ **7.** pan   **g.** measure

_____ **8.** ped   **h.** hour

_____ **9.** poly   **i.** foot

_____ **10.** prot   **j.** time

Roots that Describe Nature

Below are some Greek roots and words formed from them that are about the "natural world." You'll find these spelling words useful.

Root	Meaning	Example	Definition
anthrop	human	anthropology	study of humankind (*an* throh pol oh gee)
bio	life	biology	the study of life
dem	people	democracy	rule by the people
gen	race	genetics	study of heredity (*jen* eh tik z)
gyn	woman	gynecologist	doctor who specializes in women's health (gi nee *kol* oh jist)
helio	sun	heliotrope	sunflower (*hee* lee uh tro puh)
ichthy	fish	ichthyology	study of fish (*ik* thee ol oh gee)
ornith	bird	ornithology	study of birds (*or* neh thol oh gee)
ped	child	pediatrician	doctor who treats children (*pee* dee uh tri shun)
polit	citizen	cosmopolitan	citizen of the world
thermo	heat	thermostat	device for regulating heat
zoo	animal	zoology	study of animals

The *Auto* Root

The Greek root *auto* means "self." Many familiar spelling words are formed from it.

Word	Meaning
1. autobiography	the story of a person's life, written by that person
2. autocratic	dictatorial; with unlimited power over others
3. automatic	done without thinking
4. autopsy	examination of a dead body to find the cause of death
5. autonomy	right of self-government
6. automobile	car
7. automat	self-service restaurant
8. autograph	the name of a person in his or her own handwriting
9. automation	a system of manufacturing in which some jobs are done by machines instead of people
10. automaton	a person acting mechanically, like a robot

Quick Quiz B

Directions: Choose the word that is not spelled correctly. Spell it correctly on the lines provided for you.

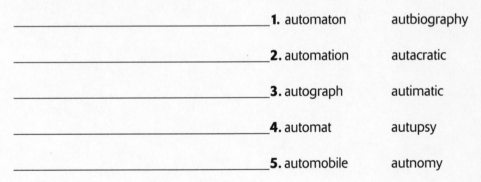

_____ **1.** automaton   autbiography

_____ **2.** automation   autacratic

_____ **3.** autograph   autimatic

_____ **4.** automat   autupsy

_____ **5.** automobile   autnomy

Answers to Quick Quizzes

Answers to Quick Quiz A

1. d

2. j

3. h

4. b

5. g

6. a

7. e

8. i

9. f

10. c

Answers to Quick Quiz B

1. autobiography

2. autocratic

3. automatic

4. autopsy

5. autonomy

Practice Test

Directions: Write **C** if the word is spelled correctly and write **X** if it is spelled incorrectly. Then write the misspelled words correctly on the lines provided for you.

_____ **1.** protatype

_____ **2.** democracy

_____ **3.** genetics

_____ **4.** horiscope

_____ **5.** chronacle

_____ **6.** cosmopolitan

_____ **7.** autograph

_____ **8.** chronology

_____ **9.** sympithy

_____ **10.** panacea

_____ **11.** telascope

_____ **12.** biology

_____ **13.** carnage

_____ **14.** gynacologist

_____ **15.** calligraphy

_____ **16.** autamobile

_____ **17.** capatal

_____ **18.** monarchy

_____ **19.** microbe

_____ **20.** arbor

Write the misspelled words correctly:

_____   _____

_____   _____

_____   _____

Answers

__X__ **1.** protatype		__X__ **11.** telascope	
__C__ **2.** democracy		__C__ **12.** biology	
__C__ **3.** genetics		__C__ **13.** carnage	
__X__ **4.** horiscope		__X__ **14.** gynacologist	
__X__ **5.** chronacle		__C__ **15.** calligraphy	
__C__ **6.** cosmopolitan		__X__ **16.** autamobile	
__C__ **7.** autograph		__X__ **17.** capatal	
__C__ **8.** chronology		__C__ **18.** monao=hy	
__X__ **9.** sympathy		__C__ **19.** microbe	
__C__ **10.** panacea		__C__ **20.** arbor	

Misspelled Words Corrected

1. prototype

4. horoscope

5. chronicle

9. sympathy

11. telescope

14. gynecologist

16. automobile

17. capital

More Word Roots | 10

As you learned in Chapter 9, roots form many common spelling words. For example, the Latin root *plac* means "pleasure." Words formed from this root include *placid, complacent, implacable, complaisant*, and *placate*.

In this chapter, you'll learn more roots.

The *Facere* Root

Many everyday spelling "demons" come from the root *facere*. You already know how to spell *fact*, one of the most common words from this root. Below are some equally useful words that are more difficult to spell. Remembering their common root, however, can help you get a handle on their spelling.

	Word	Definition
1.	faction	group of dissidents, people who take the opposing side
2.	defeat	failure
3.	factor	one of the elements that contributes to produce a result
4.	factory	a building for the manufacturing of goods
5.	facile	skilled, glib
6.	faculty	ability to do or act; staff of professors or teachers
7.	affect	pretend to have; influence
8.	infect	contaminate
9.	perfect	flawless
10.	prefect	president; head student
11.	defect	imperfection, fault
12.	factual	real or true; based on facts

Quick Quiz A

Directions: Underline the *fact* root in each of the following words. Then write each word twice to help you remember how to spell it on the lines provided for you.

1. factory _____   _____

2. perfect _____   _____

3. factor _____   _____

4. facile _____   _____

5. factual _____   _____

6. faculty _____   _____

7. defeat _____   _____

8. affect _____   _____

9. infect _____   _____

10. prefect _____   _____

11. faction _____   _____

12. defect _____   _____

Roots about Making and Moving

Below are some Latin roots that are used to form words about making and moving:

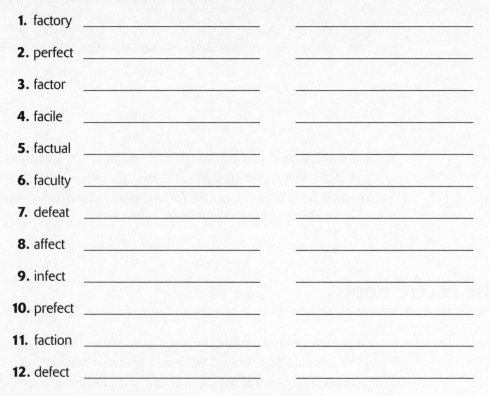

Root	Meaning	Example	Definition
dict	say	dictate	authoritative command
duct	lead	ductile	easily molded (*duk* tile)
fer	carry	transfer	carry to another place
funct	perform	functional	able to be performed
grad	go/step	degrade	go down; corrupt
ject	throw	reject	throw aside; discard
magni	large	magnify	grow larger
multi	many	multiply	increase
pel/puls	move	impel	urge
scrib	write	scribble	scrawl

Quick Quiz B

Directions: Match the root to the word. Write the letter of your choice on the lines provided for you.

_____	**1.** dict		**a.**	transfer
_____	**2.** grad		**b.**	scribble
_____	**3.** pel/puls		**c.**	magnify
_____	**4.** scrib		**d.**	dictate
_____	**5.** ject		**e.**	multiply
_____	**6.** duct		**f.**	degrade
_____	**7.** multi		**g.**	functional
_____	**8.** fer		**h.**	impel
_____	**9.** funct		**i.**	ductile
_____	**10.** magni		**j.**	reject

Quick Quiz C

Directions: Choose the word that is not spelled correctly. Spell it correctly on the lines provided for you.

1. impel   transfur   _____

2. functional   multiplie   _____

3. reject   ducktile   _____

4. ditate   scribble   _____

5. degrade   magnafy   _____

The *Tangere* Root

The root *tangere/tactus* means "to touch." The root can be spelled many different ways, including *tang-*, *tag-*, *tac-*, *ting-*, *teg-*, and *-tain*. Many useful everyday words have this root:

Word	Definition
attain	achieve, get
contact	touch
contagious	catching, communicable
contingent	dependent on unknown circumstances
disintegrate	fall apart
intact	untouched
intangible	cannot be touched; abstract
integral	essential to completeness
integrity	honesty, morality
tact	diplomacy

Quick Quiz D

Directions: Each of the following words is misspelled. Spell it correctly on the lines provided for you.

1. integrel   _____

2. tatc   _____

3. contat   _____

4. contagous   _____

5. contingant   _____

6. atain   _____

7. disintigrate   _____

8. intarct   _____

9. intangable   _____

10. integraty   _____

Roots About Amount

Study the roots, examples, and definitions. As you read, try to visualize the way the word is spelled. "See" the letters in the correct order in your mind. This will help you fix the correct spelling in your memory:

Root	Meaning	Example	Definition
alt	high	altitude	height above surface
ann	year	biennial	happening every two years (*bi* en ee al)
brev	short	abbreviation	shortened form
dors	back	dorsal	back fin
med	middle	median	in the middle (*mee* dee an)
nihil	nothing	annihilate	kill (*ann* ni ah late)
omni	all	omniscient	all-knowing (*om* nish ehnt)
pend	weigh	pendulous	hanging
sed	sit	sedate	quiet
ten	hold	tenet	belief held as true (*tehn* net)
term	end	terminal	last stop; dying
vis	see	visual	something seen (*viz* yu al)

The *Sal* Root

The Latin root *sal* means "salt." We get the word *salary* from this root. According to the story, when Roman soldiers were sent into foreign lands, they were given money to buy salt for their food. This money was called *salarium* or "salt money." Over the centuries, the word *salarium* lost all connection with salt and came to be the term we use today: *salary*.

The following important words come from the *sal* root. Some, like *sausage*, have difficult spelling patterns so read each word over several times:

Word	Definition
sausage	spicy chopped meat encased in animal intestines
sauce	fluid dressing
salad	chopped raw vegetables
saline	salty
saucy	fresh, impudent, pert
saucer	flat dish

Quick Quiz E

Directions: Write the spelling word that matches each definition on the lines provided for you. Use the words in the box below as a guide.

sausage	saucer	sauce
salad	saline	saucy

_____ **1.** chopped raw vegetables

_____ **2.** flat dish

_____ **3.** salty

_____ **4.** fresh, impudent, pert

_____ **5.** fluid dressing

_____ **6.** spicy chopped meat encased in animal intestines

Answers to Quick Quizzes

Answers to Quick Quiz A

1. <u>fact</u>ory

2. per<u>fect</u>

3. <u>fact</u>or

4. <u>fac</u>ile

5. <u>fact</u>ual

6. <u>fac</u>ulty

7. de<u>feat</u>

8. af<u>fect</u>

9. in<u>fect</u>

10. pre<u>fect</u>

11. <u>fact</u>ion

12. de<u>fect</u>

Answers to Quick Quiz B

1. d

2. f

3. h

4. b

5. j

6. i

7. e

8. a

9. g

10. c

Answers to Quick Quiz C

1. transfer

2. multiply

3. ductile

4. dictate

5. magnify

Answers to Quick Quiz D

1. integral
2. tact
3. contact
4. contagious
5. contingent
6. attain
7. disintegrate
8. intact
9. intangible
10. integrity

Answers to Quick Quiz E

1. salad
2. saucer
3. saline
4. saucy
5. sauce
6. sausage

Practice Test

Directions: Some of the following words are misspelled. Write **C** if the word is spelled correctly and write **X** if the word is spelled incorrectly. Then write the misspelled words correctly on the lines provided for you.

_____ **1.** faction

_____ **2.** disintegrate

_____ **3.** defeet

_____ **4.** factual

_____ **5.** sausage

_____ **6.** placate

_____ **7.** placid

_____ **8.** sause

_____ **9.** facile

_____ **10.** funshional

_____ **11.** integrite

_____ **12.** dictate

_____ **13.** integral

_____ **14.** altitude

_____ **15.** abbreviashion

_____ **16.** contagious

_____ **17.** magnify

_____ **18.** transfer

_____ **19.** terminal

_____ **20.** vizual

Write the misspelled words correctly:

_____   _____

_____   _____

_____   _____

Answers

   C   **1.** faction

   C   **2.** disintegrate

   X   **3.** defeet

   C   **4.** factual

   C   **5.** sausage

   C   **6.** placate

   C   **7.** placid

   X   **8.** sause

   C   **9.** facile

   X **10.** funshional

   X **11.** integrite

   C **12.** dictate

   C **13.** integral

   C **14.** altitude

   X **15.** abbreviashion

   C **16.** contagious

   C **17.** magnify

   C **18.** transfer

   C **19.** terminal

   X **20.** vizual

Misspelled Words Corrected

 3. defeat

 8. sauce

10. functional

11. integrity

15. abbreviation

20. visual

Learning *Prefixes* 11

As you learned in Chapter 9, a *prefix* is a group of letters added to the beginning of a word to change its meaning. Knowing some prefixes can help you remember how to spell many important words.

Overview of Prefixes

A *prefix* can be any number of letters, from one to many. Here are some examples:

Number of Letters	Prefix	Meaning
One-Letter Prefix	a-	not
Two-Letter Prefix	co-	with
Three-Letter Prefix	pre-	before
Four-Letter Prefix	para-	beside
Five-Letter Prefix	tract-	draw
Six-Letter Prefix	circum-	around

Prefixes are often written with a hyphen, like this: *a-*, *de-*, *re-*. The hyphen is dropped when the prefix is added to the word. Prefixes are most often attached to words without a break, like this:

Number of Letters	Prefix	Word	Meaning
One-Letter Prefix	a-	amoral	not moral (ay *mor* al)
Two-Letter Prefix	co-	cohabit	live together
Three-Letter Prefix	pre-	premature	before mature
Four-Letter Prefix	para-	paragraph	subsection of a writing
Five-Letter Prefix	tract-	tractile	able to be drawn out at length
Six-Letter Prefix	circum-	circumlocution	indirect way of speaking (sir cum loh *que* shun)

129

Attaching Prefixes

There is only one rule: Do not add or omit a letter when you attach a prefix. Here are some examples:

Prefix		Root		New Word
circum-	+	scribe	=	circumscribe
dis-	+	satisfied	=	dissatisfied
mis-	+	spell	=	misspell
un-	+	acceptable	=	unacceptable
re-	+	election	=	reelection
inter-	+	related	=	interrelated
im-	+	part	=	impart
re-	+	turn	=	return
a-	+	sexual	=	asexual
para-	+	phrase	=	paraphrase
over-	+	wrought	=	overwrought
mis-	+	cue	=	miscue
be-	+	moan	=	bemoan
over-	+	come	=	overcome
over-	+	zealous	=	overzealous

Quick Quiz A

Directions: Circle the prefix in each of the following words.

1. asexual
2. reelection
3. unacceptable
4. paraphrase
5. return
6. interrelated
7. impart
8. misspell
9. dissatisfied
10. miscue
11. overwrought
12. circumscribe

Quick Quiz B

Directions: Complete the following chart by adding prefixes to roots.

	Prefix	+	Root Word	=	New Word
1.	circum-	+	locution	=	_____
2.	co-	+	worker	=	_____
3.	dis-	+	agree	=	_____
4.	ex-	+	change	=	_____
5.	in-	+	scribe	=	_____
6.	circum-	+	navigate	=	_____
7.	re-	+	cover	=	_____
8.	a-	+	typical	=	_____
9.	epi-	+	graph	=	_____
10.	para-	+	legal	=	_____

The Prefix *Re-*

Re- means "again." It is one of the most common prefixes. Notice that all the letters of the prefix and the root word are kept when the two are combined:

Prefix	+	Root	=	Word	Definition
re-	+	absorb	=	reabsorb	absorb again
re-	+	acquaint	=	reacquaint	meet again
re-	+	qualify	=	requalify	qualify again
re-	+	admit	=	readmit	admit again
re-	+	allocate	=	reallocate	allocate again
re-	+	appear	=	reappear	appear again
re-	+	arrange	=	rearrange	change the arrangement
re-	+	attach	=	reattach	attach again
re-	+	fasten	=	refasten	fasten again
re-	+	copy	=	recopy	copy again

The Prefix *De-*

De- means "down, remove." Here are some common spelling words that begin with this prefix:

Prefix	Meaning	Example	Definition
de-	down	demolish	tear down
de-	down	dejected	discouraged
de-	down	denounce	speak against someone
de-	down	depression	sadness
de-	down	descent	moving downward
de-	remove	declaw	remove claws
de-	remove	decommission	take out of commission
de-	remove	debone	remove the bones
de-	remove	deemphasize	remove emphasis from
de-	remove	decompose	break down
de-	remove	decertify	remove certification

Quick Quiz C

Directions: Choose the word that is not spelled correctly. Spell it correctly on the lines provided for you.

1. rebsorb   decompose   _____

2. reacquaint   demphasize   _____

3. debone   dcommission   _____

4. deeclaw   requalify   _____

5. descent   reppear   _____

6. denounce   rellocate   _____

7. dejected   redmit   _____

8. deemolish   refasten   _____

9. deepression   decertify   _____

10. rerrange   reattach   _____

More Useful Prefixes

The following chart shows ten common prefixes. Each of them is used for words that you will find helpful for the GED:

Prefix	Meaning	Example	Definition
ag-	do, act	aggregate	sum total, set
ac-	to, toward	accede	agree (ak seed)
a-	not	atypical	not typical
cata-	down	catacomb	underground room
com-	with	compress	squeeze
hyper-	excessive	hyperactivity	excessive activity
hypo-	under, below	hypocrisy	false virtue (hi *pock* cra see)
sub-	under	subsistence	existing
super-	over, beyond	supercilious	arrogant (soo per *sil* e us)
ultra-	beyond	ultramarine	deep blue

Quick Quiz D

Directions: Circle the prefix in each of the following words. Then write each word twice on the lines provided for you.

1. hyperactivity _____ _____

2. supercilious _____ _____

3. aggregate _____ _____

4. compress _____ _____

5. accede _____ _____

6. hypocrisy _____ _____

7. ultramarine _____ _____

8. catacomb _____ _____

9. atypical _____ _____

10. subsistence _____ _____

Quick Quiz E

Directions: Complete the following chart by adding each prefix to its root.

Prefix	+	Root Word	=	New Word
1. sub-	+	sistence	=	_____
2. ultra-	+	marine	=	_____
3. hypo-	+	crisy	=	_____
4. cata-	+	comb	=	_____
5. hyper-	+	activity	=	_____
6. ag-	+	gregate	=	_____
7. ac-	+	cede	=	_____
8. com-	+	press	=	_____
9. super-	+	cilious	=	_____
10. a-	+	typical	=	_____

Ten Greek Prefixes

Below are ten prefixes that have made their way from ancient Greece to modern America. Read through the prefixes, meanings, and examples. Pause after each row to respell each word in your mind. This will help you remember it.

Prefix	Meaning	Example	Definition
dem-	people	democracy	government of the people
eu-	good	eulogize	speak well of someone (*yool* ee jize)
geo-	earth	geography	writing about earth
graph-	write	autograph	self-writing
hydro-	water	hydrophobia	fear of water
hyper-	over	hyperactive	excessively active
hypo-	under	hypodermic	under the skin
micro-	small	microscope	tool for looking at small objects
mis-	wrong	misspell	spell incorrectly
mono-	one	monotone	one tone

Quick Quiz F

Directions: Match each word to its prefix. Write the letter of your choice on the lines provided for you.

_____ **1.** democracy

_____ **2.** eulogize

_____ **3.** geography

_____ **4.** hydrophobia

_____ **5.** hyperactive

_____ **6.** hypodermic

_____ **7.** microscope

_____ **8.** misspell

_____ **9.** monotone

_____ **10.** autograph

a. mis

b. hydro

c. eu

d. hyper

e. micro

f. auto

g. mono

h. geo

i. hypo

j. dem

Quick Quiz G

Directions: Circle the prefix in each new spelling word. Then write the new word twice on the lines provided for you.

1. demographic _____   _____

2. euphoria   _____   _____

3. geology   _____   _____

4. graphic   _____   _____

5. hypercritical   _____   _____

6. microfilm   _____   _____

7. mistake   _____   _____

8. monotheism   _____   _____

Prefixes that Show Number

The symbols that we use for numbers—*1, 2, 3, 4,* etc.—come from Arabic. The words we use to speak or write these symbols—*one, two, three, four,* etc.—are from the Anglo-Saxons.

The following chart shows the prefixes for the numbers one to ten (1–10):

Number	Prefix	Example	Meaning
1	uni-	unicycle	cycle with one wheel
2	bi-	bicycle	cycle with two wheels
3	tri-	tripod	three-legged stand
4	quad-	quadrangle	figure with four sides and four angles
5	penta-	Pentagon	five-sided building in Virginia that houses the U.S. Department of Defense
6	hexa-	hexagon	figure with six sides
7	hepta-	heptagon	polygon with seven sides and angles
8	oct-	octet	group of eight (ock *tet*)
9	nov-	November	the ninth month in the ancient Roman calendar
10	deca-	decade	ten years

Don't forget: Correct spelling includes correct capitalization as well as having the correct letters in the correct order. The words *November* and *Pentagon* have to be capitalized because they are proper nouns. This means they name specific people, places, or things. If these words are not capitalized, they are considered misspelled.

Quick Quiz H

Directions: Match each misspelled word to its correct spelling. Write the letter of the correct spelling on the lines provided for you.

_____	**1.** unicicle	**a.**	bicycle
_____	**2.** trypod	**b.**	unicycle
_____	**3.** quadangle	**c.**	octet
_____	**4.** Pentagan	**d.**	tripod
_____	**5.** hexugon	**e.**	decade
_____	**6.** bicicle	**f.**	heptagon
_____	**7.** heptagen	**g.**	Pentagon
_____	**8.** ocket	**h.**	quadrangle
_____	**9.** Noveber	**i.**	November
_____	**10.** dekade	**j.**	hexagon

Answers to Quick Quizzes

Answers to Quick Quiz A

1. (a)sexual
2. (re) election
3. (un) acceptable
4. (para) phrase
5. (re) turn
6. (inter) related
7. (im) part
8. (mis) spell
9. (dis) satisfied
10. (mis) cue
11. (over) wrought
12. (circum) scribe

Answers to Quick Quiz B

1. circumlocution
2. coworker
3. disagree
4. exchange
5. inscribe
6. circumnavigate
7. recover
8. atypical
9. epigraph
10. paralegal

Answers to Quick Quiz C

1. reabsorb

2. deemphasize

3. decommission

4. declaw

5. reappear

6. reallocate

7. readmit

8. demolish

9. depression

10. rearrange

Answers to Quick Quiz D

1. (hyper) activity

2. (super) cilious

3. (ag) gregate

4. (com) press

5. (ac) cede

6. (hypo) crisy

7. (ultra) marine

8. (cata) comb

9. (a) typical

10. (sub) sistence

Answers to Quick Quiz E

1. subsistence

2. ultramarine

3. hypocrisy

4. catacomb

5. hyperactivity

6. aggregate

7. accede

8. compress

9. supercilious

10. atypical

Answers to Quick Quiz F

1. j

2. c

3. h

4. b

5. d

6. i

7. e

8. a

9. g

10. f

Answers to Quick Quiz G

1. (demo) graphic

2. (eu) phoria

3. (geo) logy

4. (graph) ic

5. (hyper) critical

6. (micro) film

7. (mis) take

8. (mono) theism

Answers to Quick Quiz H

1. b

2. d

3. h

4. g

5. j

6. a

7. f

8. c

9. i

10. e

Practice Test

Directions: Some of the following words are misspelled. Write **C** if the word is spelled correctly and write **X** if the word is spelled incorrectly. Then write the misspelled words correctly on the lines provided for you.

_____ **1.** premature
_____ **2.** disatisfied
_____ **3.** paragraph
_____ **4.** mispell
_____ **5.** unacceptable
_____ **6.** epidemic
_____ **7.** rearrange
_____ **8.** recopy
_____ **9.** reapear
_____ **10.** hyperactivity
_____ **11.** demolish
_____ **12.** parphrase
_____ **13.** depression
_____ **14.** hypocrisy
_____ **15.** Novamber
_____ **16.** Pentagon
_____ **17.** geography
_____ **18.** autograph
_____ **19.** microscope
_____ **20.** bicicle

Write misspelled words correctly:

_____   _____

_____   _____

_____   _____

Answers

  C **1.** premature

  X **2.** disatisfied

  C **3.** paragraph

  X **4.** mispell

  C **5.** unacceptable

  C **6.** epidemic

  C **7.** rearrange

  C **8.** recopy

  X **9.** reapear

  C **10.** hyperactivity

  C **11.** demolish

  X **12.** parphrase

  C **13.** depression

  C **14.** hypocrisy

  X **15.** Novamber

  C **16.** Pentagon

  C **17.** geography

  C **18.** autograph

  C **19.** microscope

  X **20.** bicicle

Misspelled Words Corrected

2. dissatisfied

4. misspell

9. reappear

12. paraphrase

15. November

20. bicycle

Learning *Suffixes* 12

As you learned in Chapter 9, a *suffix* is a group of words added to the end of a word to change its meaning. Knowing a few suffixes helps you remember how to spell many important words that you already know. It can also help you figure out how to spell words that are unfamiliar to you.

Overview of Suffixes

Just like with a prefix, a *suffix* can be any number of letters, from one to many. Here are some examples:

Number of Letters	Suffix	Meaning
One-Letter Suffix	-d	past tense
Two-Letter Suffix	-ty	state of being
Three-Letter Suffix	-ile	like, resembling
Four-Letter Suffix	-some	like, resembling
Five-Letter Suffix	-esque	like, resembling
Six-Letter Suffix	-aceous	having

Suffixes are always attached to the end of a word without a break. Suffixes are often written with a hyphen, like this: *-ment, -ness,* and *-tion.* The hyphen is dropped when the suffix is added to the word, like this:

Number of Letters	Suffix	Sample Word	Meaning
One-Letter Suffix	-d	gazed	looked
Two-Letter Suffix	-ty	anxiety	state of being nervous
Three-Letter Suffix	-ile	juvenile	immature
Four-Letter Suffix	-some	worrisome	distressing
Five-Letter Suffix	-esque	statuesque	shapely
Six-Letter Suffix	-aceous	curvaceous	having curves (kur *vay* shuhs)

Suffixes Determine Meaning

Adding a prefix to the front of a word changes the word's meaning. In the same way, adding a suffix to the end of a word changes a word's meaning. However, suffixes go one step further than prefixes: suffixes can affect how a word works in a sentence. That's because a suffix can determine a word's part of speech—whether the word is used as a noun, verb, adjective, or adverb. Suffixes can be used to create a verb from a noun or an adjective or an adverb from a verb, for example. Finally, suffixes can show amount or quantity.

Suffixes and Parts of Speech

Suffixes can determine a word's part of speech. For example, adding a suffix can change a word from a verb or noun to an adjective, noun, or verb. Here is an example:

verb, noun	suffix	adjective
risk	-y	risky

Suffixes and Tense

Suffixes can also change a word's *tense* (or time). For example, adding the suffix *-d* or *-ed* to the end of a word will change a present-tense verb into a past-tense verb. Adding the suffix *-ing* changes a present-tense verb into a present participle. Here are some examples:

Word	Tense	Suffix	New Word	New Tense
walk	present	-d	walked	past
skip	present	-ed	skipped	past
sleep	present	-ing	sleeping	present participle
run	present	-ing	running	present participle

Suffixes and Meaning

Suffixes can also change a word's meaning. For example, adding the suffix *-ette* (which means "little one") shows a smaller version of a person, place, or thing. Here are two examples:

Word	*Suffix*	*New Word*
kitchen	-ette	kitchenette
cigar	-ette	cigarette

Suffixes and Amount

Finally, suffixes can show amount or number. Here are some examples:

Word	*Amount*	*Suffix*	*New Word*	*Amount*
rabbit	one	s	rabbits	more than one
fox	one	es	foxes	more than one
city	one	change the *y* to *i* and add *es*	cities	more than one

As you can see, just knowing a small number of suffixes can help you spell and use many unfamiliar words.

Attaching Suffixes, Part 1

- In general, keep all the letters when you add a suffix. This is not true if the word ends in *y* or silent *e*. These cases will be discussed later:

Word		**Suffix**		**New Word**
free	+	-dom	=	freedom
neighbor	+	-hood	=	neighborhood
ski	+	-ing	=	skiing

- If the letter before the final *y* is a <u>consonant</u>, change the *y* to *i* and add the suffix:

Word		**Suffix**		**New Word**
hurry	+	-ed	=	hurried
greedy	+	-ly	=	greedily
pony	+	-es	=	ponies
query	+	-es	=	queries

Exceptions:

hurrying	shyness	dryly	
dryness	shyly	babyish	ladylike

- If the letter before the final *y* is a <u>vowel</u>, do not change the *y* before attaching a suffix:

Word		Suffix		New Word
play	+	-ing	=	playing
destroy	+	-ed	=	destroyed

Exceptions:

laid	paid	said
mislaid	underpaid	unsaid

- Drop the silent *e* if the suffix begins with a <u>vowel</u>.

Here are some examples:

Word		Suffix		New Word
write	+	-ing	=	writing
love	+	-able	=	lovable
use	+	-age	=	usage
illustrate	+	-ive	=	illustrative
argue	+	-ing	=	arguing
ache	+	-ing	=	aching
enclose	+	-sure	=	enclosure

- Keep the silent *e* if the suffix begins with a <u>consonant</u>. Here are some examples:

Word		Suffix		New Word
excite	+	-ment	=	excitement
care	+	-ful	=	careful
fierce	+	-ly	=	fiercely
sore	+	-ly	=	sorely

Exceptions:

argument	awfully	acknowledgment
duly	judgment	ninth
only	truly	wholly

- When the word ends in *ce* or *ge,* keep the *e* if the suffix begins with *a* or *e*, as in these examples:

Word		Suffix		New Word
notice	+	-able	=	noticeable
manage	+	-able	=	manageable

Exceptions:

acreage	mileage	advantageous

Quick Quiz A

Directions: Circle the suffix in each of the following words.

1. skiing
2. freedom
3. foxes
4. neighborhood
5. sleeping

6. cigarette
7. kitchenette
8. ladylike
9. risky
10. skipping

Quick Quiz B

Directions: Complete the following chart by adding suffixes to roots and place your answer on the lines provided for you.

Root Word	Suffix	New Word
1. accidental +	-ly =	_____
2. mercy +	-ful =	_____
3. decay +	-ed =	_____
4. drunken +	-ness =	_____
5. foolhardy +	-ness =	_____
6. pacify +	-ed =	_____

Quick Quiz C

Directions: Choose the word that is not spelled correctly. Spell it correctly on the lines provided for you.

1. writing   aching   sorly _____
2. lovable   judgment   arguement _____
3. usaege   lying   fiercely _____
4. dying   excitement   truely _____
5. careful   nineth   duly _____
6. arguing   acknowledgment   noticable _____

Attaching Suffixes, Part 2

- If the word ends in *ie*, change the *ie* to *y* before adding *ing*:

Word		Suffix		New Word
lie	+	-ing	=	lying
tie	+	-ing	=	tying

- Add *-ly* to change an adjective to an adverb. Here are some examples:

Word		Suffix		New Word
brave	+	-ly	=	bravely
calm	+	-ly	=	calmly

  Exception: If the adjective ends in *ic,* add *al* before *-ly*:

Word		al		Suffix		New Word
drastic	+	-al	+	-ly	=	drastically
scientific	+	-al	+	-ly	=	scientifically

  Exception: If the adjective ends in *-ble,* change *-ble* to *-bly*:

Word	New Word
able	ably
noble	nobly

- In a one-syllable word, double the final consonant before a suffix beginning with a vowel:

Word		Suffix		New Word
plan	+	-er	=	planner
big	+	-est	=	biggest
stop	+	-ed	=	stopped

  Exception: Don't double the final consonant if it comes after two vowels or another consonant. For example: *failed, stooped, warmer,* and *lasting*.

- In a word of two or more syllables, double the final consonant only if it is in an accented syllable before a suffix beginning with a vowel. For example:

Word	Suffix		New Word
deFER	+	-ed	=	deferred
resubMIT	+	-ing	=	resubmitting

Exceptions: The rule does not apply if the final consonant comes right after two vowels:

Word	Suffix		New Word
ObTAIN	+	-ed	=	obtained
conCEAL	+	-ing	=	concealing

Exceptions: The rule does not apply if the final consonant comes right after another consonant:

Word	Suffix		New Word
AbDUCT	+	-ing	=	abducting
comMEND	+	-ed	=	commending

Exceptions: The rule does not apply if the accent shifts back to the first syllable:

Word	Suffix		New Word
reFER	+	-ence	=	REFerence
preFER	+	-ence	=	PREFerence
conFER	+	-ence	=	CONference

- If a words ends in *ic,* insert a *k* after the *c* before adding *-ed*, *-er*, *-ing*, or *-y.*

Word	Suffix		New Word
mimic	+	-ing	=	mimicking
traffic	+	-ing	=	trafficking
frolic	+	-ing	=	frolicking

Quick Quiz D

Directions: Complete the following by adding suffixes to roots and place your answer on the lines provided for you.

Root		Suffix		New Word
1. untie	+	-ing	=	_____
2. lie	+	-ing	=	_____
3. brave	+	-ly	=	_____
4. usual	+	-ly	=	_____
5. probable	+	-ly	=	_____
6. due	+	-ly	=	_____
7. grin	+	-ing	=	_____
8. shop	+	-ed	=	_____
9. fail	+	-ed	=	_____
10. last	+	-ing	=	_____

Quick Quiz E

Directions: Circle the suffix in each new spelling word. Then write each word twice on the lines provided for you.

1. deferred   _____   _____

2. trafficking   _____   _____

3. obtained   _____   _____

4. concealing   _____   _____

5. conference   _____   _____

Attaching Suffixes, Part 3

- Adding -*able and* -*ible*

  An adjective usually ends in -*able* rather than -*ible* if you can trace the word back to a noun ending in -*ation*:

Adjective	*Noun*
adaptable	adaptation
alterable	alteration

  Exceptions: predictable, correctable

  When the word ends in -*ce* or -*ge* with a soft sound, keep the *e* before -*able*. This keeps the soft sound, as in *peaceable* and *changeable*. When the -*ce* or -*ge* are hard, drop the *e*, as in *implacable*, *practicable*, and *despicable*.

  There are more -*able* words than -*ible*, so if you're in a pressure situation, go with -*able*. The following chart lists some of the most important spelling words that fall under this category:

-*able*	-*ible*
acceptable	accessible
adaptable	admissible
amiable	audible
appreciable	collapsible
believable	collectible
breakable	contemptible
changeable	comprehensible
charitable	credible
correctable	digestible
debatable	discernible
desirable	eligible
despicable	flexible
enviable	feasible
excusable	gullible
favorable	intelligible
fixable	invincible
incurable	legible
lovable	ostensible
manageable	repressible
measurable	resistible
memorable	sensible
peaceable	tangible
predictable	visible
preferable	
profitable	
reliable	
sociable	
usable	
workable	

- Verbs ending in *-ate* usually become nouns ending in *-or* rather than *-er*:

Verb	Noun
create	creator
indicate	indicator

- In general, spell an adjective with *-ant* rather than *-ent* if you can trace it to a noun that ends in *-ancy* or *ance*:

Noun	Adjective
brilliance	brilliant
vacancy	vacant

Spell an adjective with *-ent* rather than *-ant* if you can trace it to a noun ending in *ence* or *ency*:

Noun	Adjective
independence	independent
decency	decent

The following chart summarizes the most often misspelled *-ant/-ent* words:

-ance/-ancy	*-ence/-ency*
abundance	adherence
assistance	adolescence
attendance	antecedent
compliance	coherence
defiance	convalescence
extravagance	correspondence
fragrance	currency
ignorance	eloquence
lieutenant	fluency
observance	frequency
reliance	intelligence
reluctance	permanence
resistance	potency
significance	recurrence
truancy	urgency

Quick Quiz F

Directions: Write the words formed by adding the suffix *-able* or *–ible* on the lines provided for you.

1. sens_____
2. memor_____
3. work_____
4. gull_____
5. believe_____

6. feas_____
7. collect_____
8. cred_____
9. use_____
10. love_____

Quick Quiz G

Directions: Complete each word by filling in *ance/-ancy* or *-ence/-ency* on the lines provided for you.

1. fragr_____
2. truant_____
3. intellig_____

4. reluct_____
5. urgent_____
6. ignor_____

Answers to Quick Quizzes

Answers to Quick Quiz A

1. ski (ing)

2. free (dom)

3. fox (es)

4. neighbor (hood)

5. sleep (ing)

6. cigar (ette)

7. kitchen (ette)

8. lady (like)

9. risk (y)

10. skipp (ing)

Answers to Quick Quiz B

1. accidentally

2. merciful

3. decayed

4. drunkenness

5. foolhardiness

6. pacified

Answers to Quick Quiz C

1. sorely

2. argument

3. usage

4. truly

5. ninth

6. noticeable

Answers to Quick Quiz D

1. untying
2. lying
3. bravely
4. usually
5. probably
6. duly
7. grinning
8. shopped
9. failed
10. lasting

Answers to Quick Quiz E

1. deferr(ed)
2. traffick(ing)
3. obtain(ed)
4. conceal(ing)
5. confer(ence)

Answers to Quick Quiz F

1. sensible
2. memorable
3. workable
4. gullible
5. believable
6. feasible
7. collectible
8. credible
9. usable
10. lovable

Answers to Quick Quiz G

1. fragrance
2. truancy
3. intelligence
4. reluctance
5. urgency
6. ignorance

Practice Test

Directions: Match each misspelled word to its correct spelling. Write the letter of the correct spelling on the lines provided for you.

_____ **1.** changable

_____ **2.** cigaratte

_____ **3.** carful

_____ **4.** visable

_____ **5.** argueing

_____ **6.** anxietie

_____ **7.** independant

_____ **8.** statuesqy

_____ **9.** decayd

_____ **10.** drily

_____ **11.** juvenale

_____ **12.** nineth

_____ **13.** concealling

_____ **14.** writting

_____ **15.** bravelly

a. anxiety

b. juvenile

c. statuesque

d. cigarette

e. dryly

f. ninth

g. writing

h. careful

i. decayed

j. arguing

k. bravely

l. changeable

m. visible

n. independent

o. concealing

Answers

1. l
2. d
3. h
4. m
5. j
6. a
7. n
8. c
9. i
10. e
11. b
12. f
13. o
14. g
15. k

Words Commonly Confused

Words Often Misspelled | 13

Some English words do not follow the spelling patterns that you have been learning. They do not follow spelling rules, either. For this reason, they are often misspelled. In this chapter, you will learn some of these important words and helpful ways to remember how to spell them.

Create a Memory Trigger

One good way to remember a tough spelling word is to create a memory link. For example, you can remember that *all right* is two words because it is the opposite of *all wrong*. Here are a few more well-known difficult spelling words and their memory triggers:

- *Dessert* has two *s*'s like "strawberry shortcake."
- The *principal* of a school is your <u>pal</u>.
- *Friend* ends in <u>end</u> because I will be your fri<u>end</u> until the <u>end</u>.
- The word <u>ran</u> is in *errand* and we <u>ran</u> an er<u>ran</u>d.
- So you don't confuse *there* and *their*, remember that *here* and *there* tell of places.

Try to create a way to link each of the following words in your memory. For example, you might make up a poem, song, or chant that helps you remember the order of tricky letters.

again	once
remember	together
believe	fourth
tired	sure
different	decide

161

Quick Quiz A

Directions: Match each misspelled word to its correct spelling. Write the letter of the correct spelling on the lines provided for you.

_____**1.** diferent   **a.** tired

_____**2.** togeter   **b.** believe

_____**3.** deside   **c.** different

_____**4.** beleive   **d.** again

_____**5.** onse   **e.** fourth

_____**6.** forthe   **f.** together

_____**7.** tirde   **g.** remember

_____**8.** rember   **h.** once

_____**9.** soore   **i.** decide

_____**10.** agin   **j.** sure

Look for Letter Patterns

Some people have nicknamed these difficult spelling words "demons." That's because they often baffle people who have not studied them! Now that you have been warned, you won't be fooled by these spelling words.

As you read these words, underline the letter patterns that you find difficult to remember. Underlining them will help you fix the correct order of letters in your mind:

1. shoe   6. tear

2. April   7. across

3. many   8. ready

4. sincerely   9. disappear

5. truly   10. business

Quick Quiz B

Directions: Write the spelling word that matches each definition on the lines provided for you. Use the words in the box as your guide.

shoe	tear	April	across
many	ready	sincerely	disappear
truly	business		

1. really _____

2. nine letter word used at the end of a letter _____

3. foot covering _____

4. month after March _____

5. several _____

6. company _____

7. vanish _____

8. rip _____

9. opposite from _____

10. all set to go _____

Say Words Correctly

Many words are misspelled because the writer misses a sound or a syllable. Unstressed vowels and syllables are very often the cause. For example, *miniature* is often misspelled without the second "i" because it is pronounced as *min-a-tur,* rather than as *min-ia-ture.*

Take a few moments to pronounce the following often-mispronounced spelling demons. This will help you learn to spell them correctly:

1. accidentally
2. Arctic
3. diamond
4. eighth
5. lightning
6. none
7. original
8. recognize
9. symptom
10. umbrella

Quick Quiz C

Directions: Spell each of these words correctly on the lines provided for you. Look for mistakes in missed sounds or syllables. The sound may be missing or it may be in the wrong place in the word.

1. symtom _____

2. dimond _____

3. eigth _____

4. umbrela _____

5. litning _____

6. noone _____

7. Artic _____

8. origanal _____

9. reconize _____

10. accidently _____

Divide a Word into Its Parts

Another good way to master tricky words is to break them down into smaller parts. See how you can divide the following words to make them easier to remember how to spell:

1. February
2. until
3. heard
4. guess
5. instead
6. hundred
7. probably
8. answer
9. acknowledge
10. interesting

Quick Quiz D

Directions: Write each word three times on the lines provided for you. This will help you remember it.

1. February   _____ _____ _____

2. until   _____ _____ _____

3. heard   _____ _____ _____

4. guess   _____ _____ _____

5. instead   _____ _____ _____

6. hundred   _____ _____ _____

7. probably   _____ _____ _____

8. answer   _____ _____ _____

9. acknowledge _____ _____ _____

10. interesting   _____ _____ _____

Classify Errors

You can also "classify" errors to make it easier for you to concentrate on the words that are hard for you to spell. To do this, just figure out what words give you the most trouble and concentrate on them. For example, if you have a problem with words that contain *ie/ei*, study the *ie/ei* rule and concentrate on the words that follow the rules and the major exceptions. Try it with the following ten words:

1. maybe
2. because
3. friend
4. enough
5. address
6. beautiful
7. through
8. ache
9. calendar
10. crowd

Quick Quiz E

Directions: Choose the word that is not spelled correctly. Spell it correctly on the lines provided for you.

1. maybe	red	sincerly	_____
2. because	calandar	decide	_____
3. crod	remember	ready	_____
4. ake	once	disappear	_____
5. through	beleeve	business	_____
6. adress	shoe	many	_____
7. enough	agan	across	_____
8. beeutiful	different	truly	_____
9. freind	together	fourth	_____
10. Arctic	umbrela	diamond	_____

Guess and Check

To check the spelling of an unfamiliar or tricky word, make a guess. Write the word down and see how it looks. Sometimes, you will be able to see if you have spelled the word correctly. If you misspelled it, you might be able to see where you made the mistake: perhaps you added a letter or left one off. You can even try two or three different ways to spell the word. If you are still unsure about the spelling, check the word in a dictionary. Try it now with these twenty words:

1.	kindergarten	**11.**	holiday
2.	hurricane	**12.**	length
3.	gorgeous	**13.**	ingredient
4.	landscape	**14.**	generous
5.	magnet	**15.**	label
6.	guard	**16.**	vegetable
7.	maintain	**17.**	marriage
8.	knowledge	**18.**	genuine
9.	immigrate	**19.**	Illinois
10.	forward	**20.**	hemisphere

Quick Quiz F

Directions: Some of the following words are misspelled. Write **C** if the underlined word is spelled correctly and write **X** if it is spelled incorrectly. Then write the misspelled words correctly on the lines provided for you.

_____**1.** gorgous		_____**6.** vegatable	
_____**2.** genine		_____**7.** imigrate	
_____**3.** legnth		_____**8.** marriage	
_____**4.** guard		_____**9.** ingredient	
_____**5.** hurricane		_____**10.** hemesphere	

Write the misspelled words correctly:

_____   _____

_____   _____

_____   _____

Proofreading

In this chapter, you learned tips for spelling difficult words. Let's expand that to include proofreading for spelling errors. How good is your eye for misspellings when they appear in a printed passage? Read the following passage and circle all the misspelled words. Then spell the words correctly in the spaces provided. Look for homonyms, silent letters, and missing letters. Don't forget to apply spelling rules, too! Check the answer key for your score.

Baseball

Their have been many controvercial World Series, but the most imfamous was certainly the throne World Series of 1919. Even though the White Sox were favored five to one, about 2 millon dollars had been bet on the Cincinnati Reds to win. Sensing a sure thing, Jack Doyle, the head of a New York City beting ring, rigged the series. Actually, the series seemed quiet respectable, with the Reds winning it five games to three. For this reason, very few people suspected the players had been bought. Neverless, the very next day sportswriter Hugh Fullerton suggested that something was not quite right. As a result of Fullerton's suggestion, the owner of the White Sox, Charles Comiskey, offered a cash reward to anyone who could prove a fix. It took allmost a year for three men—Lefty Williams, Eddie Cicotte, and "Shoeless" Joe Jackson—to sign confessions admitting the series had been fixed and they were in on it. But just before the trail was scheduled to start, the confessions mysteriously vanished from the office of the Illinois State Attorney. When the case was finally tried, the three men denied having made any confessions and having been involved in any way in the rigging scheme because there was no proof against them.

1. _____

2. _____

3. _____

4. _____

5. _____

6. _____

7. _____

8. _____

9. _____

10. _____

Answers

1. there
2. controversial
3. infamous
4. thrown
5. million
6. betting
7. quite
8. nevertheless
9. almost
10. trial

Try it again with the following paragraph. Read the passage, circle all the misspelled words, and spell the words correctly in the spaces provided for you.

The Potato

The potatoe has had a major historical inpact on the country of Ireland. In the eighteenth and nintheenth centurys, the average Irish citizen planted potatoes and ate about ten pounds of potatoes a day—and little else. Potatoes are nourishing: on this deit, the Irish population nearly tripled from the middle of the eighteenth century to just about the middle of the nineteenth century. But depending on only one food was dangerous. When the potato blite hit Europe in 1845, the results were devestating in Ireland. In Ireland, the potato famine meant more than starvation that year. It meant no sede potatoes to use to grow the next year's crop. It meant that the pig or cow that would usaully have been sold to pay the rent had to be slaughtered, because there was nothing to faten it on. No pig or cow meant no rent. No rent meant eviction. As a result, homelessness and disease followed on the heels of hunger. Almost a million Irish people died as a result of the potato blight. Another million moved to the United States.

1. _____
2. _____
3. _____
4. _____
5. _____
6. _____
7. _____
8. _____
9. _____
10. _____

Answers

1. potato
2. impact
3. nineteenth
4. centuries
5. diet
6. blight
7. devastating
8. seed
9. usually
10. fatten

Answers to Quick Quizzes

Answers to Quick Quiz A

1. c

2. f

3. i

4. b

5. h

6. e

7. a

8. g

9. j

10. d

Answers to Quick Quiz B

1. truly

2. sincerely

3. shoe

4. April

5. many

6. business

7. disappear

8. tear

9. across

10. ready

Answers to Quick Quiz C

1. symptom

2. diamond

3. eighth

4. umbrella

5. lightning

6. none

7. Arctic

8. original

9. recognize

10. accidentally

Answers to Quick Quiz E

1. sincerely
2. calendar
3. crowd
4. ache
5. believe
6. address
7. again
8. beautiful
9. friend
10. umbrella

Answers to Quick Quiz F

__X__	**1.** gorgous		__X__	**6.** vegatable
__X__	**2.** genine		__X__	**7.** imigrate
__X__	**3.** legnth		__C__	**8.** marriage
__C__	**4.** guard		__C__	**9.** ingredient
__C__	**5.** hurricane		__X__	**10.** hemesphere

Misspelled Words Corrected

1. gorgeous
2. genuine
3. length
6. vegetable
7. immigrate
10. hemisphere

Practice Test

Directions: Some of the following words are misspelled. Write **C** if the word is spelled correctly and write **X** if the word is spelled incorrectly. Then write the misspelled words correctly on the lines provided for you.

_____**1.** sincerly

_____**2.** deside

_____**3.** fourth

_____**4.** believe

_____**5.** remember

_____**6.** truely

_____**7.** business

_____**8.** Febuary

_____**9.** symptom

_____**10.** Arctic

_____**11.** guess

_____**12.** origanal

_____**13.** lightning

_____**14.** holaday

_____**15.** ingredient

Write the misspelled words correctly:

_____   _____

_____   _____

_____

Answers

    X   **1.** sincerly

    X   **2.** deside

    C   **3.** fourth

    C   **4.** believe

    C   **5.** remember

    X   **6.** truely

    C   **7.** business

    X   **8.** Febuary

    C   **9.** symptom

    C **10.** Arctic

    C **11.** guess

    X **12.** origanal

    C **13.** lightning

    X **14.** holaday

    C **15.** ingredient

Misspelled Words Corrected

1. sincerely

2. decide

6. truly

8. February

12. original

14. holiday

Commonly Confused Words 14

Some pairs of words sound or look very much alike. However, they do not have the same meanings. Some of these words are different parts of speech. Some can be nouns and others can be verbs, for example. Others can be adjectives or adverbs, too. When you write one of these words, look carefully to make sure you have written the word you want to use.

We have special names for these commonly confused words: *homonyms* and *homophones*.

- *Homonyms* are words with the same spelling and pronunciations but different meanings. Examples:

Word	Meaning	Word	Meaning
bore	pest, nuisance (noun)	lie	falsehood (noun)
bore	caliber (noun)	lie	to tell a falsehood (verb)
bore	drill (verb)	lie	place down (verb)
bore	annoy (verb)		

- *Homophones* are words with the same pronunciation but different spellings and meanings. Examples:

Word	Meaning	Word	Meaning
heir	beneficiary	hear	listen
air	atmosphere	here	in this place
err	make a mistake		

Ten Often Confused Words

Here are ten words that people often misuse. Some are pairs, but a few come in threes and even fours! Each word within a group has the same pronunciation:

Word	Meaning	Part of Speech
1. air	atmosphere	noun
err	to make a mistake	verb
2. a lot	many	adverb
allot	divide	verb
3. altar	platform for religious rites	noun
alter	change	verb
4. allowed	given permission	verb
aloud	out loud, verbally	adverb
5. are	form of "to be"	verb
our	belonging to us	pronoun
6. bare	undressed	adjective
bare	unadorned, plain	adjective
bear	animal	noun
bear	carry, hold	verb
7. born	native, natural	adjective
borne	endured	verb
8. bore	tiresome person	noun
boar	male pig	noun
9. brake	device for slowing a vehicle	noun
break	to crack or destroy	verb
10. breadth	measurement	noun
breath	inhalation and exhalation	noun

Quick Quiz A

Directions: Choose the correct word to complete each sentence.

1. The priest placed the prayer book on the (alter, altar).

2. Do you think I was (born, borne) yesterday?

3. The vase is very fragile and can (break, brake) easily.

4. Smoky the (Bare, Bear) warns us not to start forest fires

5. No one under 18 is (allowed, aloud) in the club.

6. People deserve (allot, a lot) of credit for studying for their GED.

7. The dog's (breadth, breath) was smelly.

8. My date was such a (bore, boar) that he put even himself to sleep.

9. The (air, err) in the locker room smelled of old socks.

10. We gave (are, our) old clothes to the charity.

Five More Confusing Words

Below are five more word pairs that are confusing. As a result, they are often misspelled and misused:

Word	*Meaning*
1. all together	all at one time
altogether	completely
2. already	previously
all ready	completely prepared
3. arc	part of the circumference of a circle; curved line
ark	boat
4. ascent	to move up
assent	to agree
5. base	the bottom part of an object; the plate in baseball; morally low
bass	the lowest male voice; a type of fish; a musical in-strument

Quick Quiz B

Directions: Match each word to its meaning. Then, write the letter of the answer on the lines provided for you.

_____**1.** all ready   **a.** all at one time

_____**2.** ark   **b.** completely prepared

_____**3.** assent   **c.** completely

_____**4.** arc   **d.** type of fish

_____**5.** base   **e.** boat

_____**6.** bass   **f.** to move up

_____**7.** already   **g.** morally low

_____**8.** all together   **h.** to agree

_____**9.** ascent   **i.** previously

_____**10.** altogether   **j.** curved line

Ten More Tricky Words

Do you know the difference between *hangar* and *hanger*? A *hangar* is an airplane garage. A *hanger* is a wire tool used for hanging clothing in a closet. Below are ten more words that are often confused because they sound alike:

Word	*Meaning*
1. beau	sweetheart
bow	device used to propel arrows
	loops of ribbon
2. berth	sleeping area in a ship
birth	being born
3. board	thin piece of wood
	group of directors
bored	not interested
4. bread	baked goods
bred	to cause to be born (past participle of "to breed")
5. bridal	about a bride or a wedding
bridle	part of a horse's harness
6. buy	to purchase
by	near or next to
7. capital	city or town that is the official seat of government
	highly important
	net worth of a business
Capitol	the building in Washington, D.C., where the U.S. Congress meets
8. peer	person of equal standing
	to look at closely
pier	a structure extending into a body of water
9. cell	a small room, as in a convent or a prison
sell	to trade
10. cent	a penny
scent	smell

Six Confusing Word Pairs

People often confuse the spelling of *clothes* and *cloths*. That's because the two words sound so much alike. *Clothes* are garments that we wear, clothing. *Cloths* are pieces of fabric. As you can see, the words have very different meanings. Below are six more words that sound the same but do not mean the same thing at all. Study these words so you can use them correctly in all your written documents, not just the GED:

1. *cheep*: what a bird says   *cheap*: not expensive

2. *deer* : animal   *dear* : beloved

3. *dessert*: sweets at the end of a meal   *desert*: dry region

4. *do*: act or make (verb)   *due*: caused by (adjective)

5. *dye*: change color   *die*: cease living

6. *carat*: unit of weight in gemstones   *carrot*: vegetable

Quick Quiz C

Directions: Underline the correct definition for each word in *italics*.

1. *dry region*   dessert   desert

2. *change color*   die   dye

3. *vegetable*   carat   carrot

4. *beloved*   deer   dear

5. *not expensive*   cheep   cheap

6. *act or make* (verb)   due   do

7. *sweets at the end of a meal*   dessert   desert

8. *what a bird says*   cheap   cheep

9. *animal*   deer   dear

10. *cease living*   die   dye

Five Tricky Word Groups

Cite, site, and *sight* are all pronounced the same way: SITE. However, each word has a very different meaning. To *cite* something is to quote it. As you can tell, *cite* is used as a verb. A *site* (a noun) is a place. *Sight* has four meanings: (1) a view, (2) eyesight, (3) something that looks very strange or funny, or (4) a device on a gun or telescope that helps you aim it. Below are ten more word groups that sound the same but have vastly different meanings:

Word	Definition	Part of Speech
1. cede	yield	verb
seed	kernel	noun
2. compliment	praise	noun, verb
complement	remainder, addition	noun
3. descent	go down	noun
dissent	conflict	noun
4. discreet	careful; able to keep secrets	adjective
discrete	single	adjective
5. elicit	draw out	verb
illicit	illegal	adjective

Quick Quiz D

Directions: Choose the correct word to complete each sentence.

1. The child blushed at the lovely (compliment, complement) about her outfit.
2. People who can keep secrets are (discrete, discreet).
3. The robber was clearly involved in (illicit, elicit) activities.
4. We planted the avocado (seed, cede) in the backyard.
5. The (descent, dissent) in the submarine made our ears pop.
6. How can you best (elicit, illicit) information from someone unwilling to talk?
7. A red scarf is a good (compliment, complement) to a black jacket.
8. The speaker refused to (cede, seed) the microphone to another speaker.
9. The (descent, dissent) was so strong that we knew the tax increase would never pass.
10. Place the pills in (discreet, discrete) containers so they don't get mixed up.

Answers to Quick Quizzes

Answers to Quick Quiz A

1. altar

2. born

3. break

4. Bear

5. allowed

6. a lot

7. breath

8. bore

9. air

10. our

Answers to Quick Quiz B

1. b

2. e

3. h

4. j

5. g

6. d

7. i

8. a

9. f

10. c

Answers to Quick Quiz C

1. *dry region*: <u>desert</u>

2. *change color* : <u>dye</u>

3. *vegetable*: <u>carrot</u>

4. *beloved*: <u>dear</u>

5. *not expensive*: <u>cheap</u>

6. *act or make* (verb): <u>do</u>

7. *sweets at the end of a meal*: <u>dessert</u>

8. *what a bird says* : <u>cheep</u>

9. *animal*: <u>deer</u>

10. *cease living*: <u>die</u>

Answers to Quick Quiz D

1. compliment

2. discreet

3. illicit

4. seed

5. descent

6. elicit

7. complement

8. cede

9. dissent

10. discrete

Practice Test

Directions: Match each word to its meaning. Write the letter of the meaning on the lines provided for you.

_____ **1.** alter

_____ **2.** bore

_____ **3.** air

_____ **4.** lie

_____ **5.** heir

_____ **6.** err

_____ **7.** allot

_____ **8.** a lot

_____ **9.** hear

_____ **10.** here

a. make a mistake

b. atmosphere

c. many

d. to change

e. in this place

f. divide

g. pest, nuisance

h. listen

i. beneficiary

j. untrue statement

Directions: Unscramble each word to match its meaning. Then write the word on the lines provided for you.

Word	Meaning	Unscrambled Word
11. rae	form of "to be"	_____
uor	belonging to us	_____
12. abre	undressed	_____
ebar	animal	_____
13. obrn	native, natural	_____
orbne	endured	_____
14. rboe	tiresome person	_____
obar	male pig	_____
15. abrke	slows a car	_____
rebak	to crack or destroy	_____
16. rca	curved line	_____
rak	boat	_____
17. asbe	bottom part	_____
abss	musical instrument	_____
18. ebau	sweetheart	_____
obw	loops of ribbon	_____
19. erbth	sleeping area in a ship	_____
irtbh	being born	_____
20. rbead	baked goods	_____
redb	to cause to be born	_____

Answers

1. d

2. g

3. b

4. j

5. i

6. a

7. f

8. c

9. h

10. e

11. are, our

12. bare, bear

13. born, borne

14. bore, boar

15. brake, break

16. arc, ark

17. base, bass

18. beau, bow

19. berth, birth

20. bread, bred

More Commonly Confused Words

15

As you learned in Chapter 14, some pairs of words sound or look very much alike. Some pairs (or groups) of words are spelled the exact same way, like *bow* (a ribbon) and *bow* (the front of a ship). The first "bow" is pronounced BO. The second "bow" is pronounced BOU. As you can tell, these two words look exactly the same, but they have very different pronunciations and meanings.

Other pairs or groups of words are spelled differently but have the same sound. They have different meanings, however. This is true of the words *to*, *two*, and *too*. All three words are pronounced TOO:

- *To* means "toward."
- *Two* means "2" or "a pair."
- *Too* means "also."

It's very important to learn to distinguish between these words so you can express your exact meaning on the GED. It's also important to learn these words so you use them the correct way in all your writing. In this chapter, you will learn more pairs and groups of confusing words.

Six Confusing Word Pairs

Perhaps you have seen the word *glutinous* on a menu in a Chinese or Asian restaurant. It's most often used as an adjective with rice. When you see *glutinous rice*, it means sticky rice. There's a word that sounds the same as *glutinous* but has a very different meaning: *gluttonous*. It means "eating a lot."

Below are six more word pairs that are often confused because they sound alike. As you read the words, read the sentences to help you remember them:

Word	Meaning	Sentence
1. faint	pass out	Some people *faint* from stress.
feint	trick	The boxer tricked his opponent with a *feint*.
2. fare	price for transporting	The bus *fare* is $1.25 a passenger.
fair	not biased	The test was *fair*.
	moderately large	It was a *fair* portion of meat.
	moderately good	The food was *fair*, not great.
3. faze	to stun	The sight of his blue hair *fazed* her.
phase	a stage in life	He's just going through a *phase*.
4. for	because	You must study, *for* it will help you pass.
four	the number 4	The test had *four* parts.
5. flour	milled wheat	The recipe calls for a cup of *flour*.
flower	blossom	Marta had a beautiful *flower* garden.
6. gorilla	ape	We saw the *gorilla* at the zoo.
guerrilla	type of soldier	The *guerrilla* shot his gun in the battle.

Quick Quiz A

Directions: Unscramble each word to match its meaning. Then write the word on the lines provided for you.

Word	Meaning	Unscrambled Word
1. ofur	the number 4	_____
orf	because	_____
2. hpase	a stage in life	_____
azef	to stun	_____
3. aifnt	pass out	_____
einft	trick	_____
4. aifr	not biased	_____
afre	the price charged for transporting a passenger	_____
5. lofur	milled wheat	_____
lowfer	blossom	_____
6. uegrrilla	type of soldier	_____
origlla	ape	_____

Five More Confusing Word Pairs

The word *blue* is the color. The word *blew* is the past tense of "to blow." The words sound the same, but are spelled differently and have different meanings. Below are five more tricky word pairs. Read the sentences that follow each word. These will help you learn how to use the words correctly in your writing.

1. *grate*: irritate, reduce to small pieces

    The cook likes to *grate* carrots into the salad.

    great: large amount, enthusiastic, considerable, excellent

    We traveled a *great* distance to the test site.

    Luke is a *great* reader.

    The party was a *great* surprise.

    We had a *great* time at the circus.

2. *guilt*: blame

    Guilt can linger, like shame and remorse.

    gilt: thin gold covering

    The *gilt* bracelet glittered in the sunlight.

3. *hall*: entryway

    The guests left their muddy shoes in the *hall*.

    haul: to drag

    We had to *haul* the boxes because they were too heavy to carry.

4. *hair*: the stuff on your head and body

    The middle-aged man was dismayed to find his *hair* falling out.

    heir: beneficiary of an estate

    Rick was the *heir* of his parents' estate so he inherited everything.

5. *heard*: listened

    I *heard* what he said, even though he spoke softly.

    herd: group of animals

    The *herd* of animals kicked up a lot of dust.

Groups of Animals

We use the word *herd* to describe a general group of animals. However, there are specialized words for animal groups. Here are some of the most common ones. Multiple meanings are noted where they apply:

Word	*Animal Group*	*Multiple Meaning*
brood	chickens	*brood* also means "to sulk"
covey	game birds	
drove	sheep or oxen	*drove* is also the past tense of "to drive."
flock	birds	*flocking* is also a type of embroidery
gaggle	geese	
gam	whales	*gam* is a slang word for "legs"
murder	crows	*murder* also means "to kill"
pride	lions	*pride* also means "self-esteem"
school	fish	*school* also means "educational institution"
stable	horses	*stable* also means "steady, fixed"
swarm	bees	*swarm* also means to "crowd"

Quick Quiz B

Directions: Write the definition of each of the following words on the lines provided for you.

1. heard: _____

  herd: _____

2. hall: _____

  haul: _____

3. grate: _____

  great: _____

4. hair: _____

  heir: _____

5. guilt: _____

  gilt: _____

Possessive Pronouns vs. Contractions

Many people confuse possessive pronouns and contractions because they sound the same. For example:

- *it's* is the contraction for "it is."

  You use it like this: *It's* a sunny day.

- *its* is the possessive pronoun

  You use it like this: The dog wagged *its* tail.

  Study the chart below:

Possessive Pronouns	Contractions
its	it's (it is)
your	you're (you are)
their	they're (they are)
whose	who's (who is)

Additional Confusing Word Pairs

A *beet* (noun) is a vegetable. It's a round bulb with a pretty reddish purple color and a sweet taste. A *beat* (noun) is the rhythm of a piece of music or poetry. To *beat* (verb) is to strike. Below are five more word pairs with confusing spellings because of their identical sounds:

Word	Meaning	Part of Speech
1. here	in this place	adverb
hear	listen	verb
2. hole	crater, opening	noun
whole	entire	adjective
3. hours	60 minutes	noun
ours	belonging to us	pronoun
4. knew	past tense of "to know"	verb
new	not old	adjective
5. leech	bloodsucking worm	noun
leach	to dissolve	verb

Quick Quiz C

Directions: Circle the correct definition for each word in *italics*.

1. *leech*	entire	to dissolve	bloodsucking worm
2. *hole*	entire	crater	60 minutes
3. *here*	listen	in this place	not old
4. *hours*	belonging to us	60 minutes	crater
5. *knew*	not old	past tense of "to know"	listen
6. *hear*	listen	belonging to us	blame
7. *whole*	crater, opening	not old	entire
8. *ours*	blame	60 minutes	belonging to us
9. *new*	not old	past tense of "to know"	to drag
10. *leach*	bloodsucking worm	to dissolve	whales

A Dozen Confusing Word Pairs

Stationary means "not moving." *Stationery* is writing paper. Below are twelve other word pairs that present special problems to writers. As you read these words, make up a sentence to use each one. That will help you remember how to use the words correctly:

1. *lead*: to conduct; bluish-gray metal	*led*: past tense of "to lead"
2. *lesson*: instruction, lecture	*lessen*: to reduce
3. *maid*: a female servant	*made*: did
4. *meat*: animal flesh	*meet*: encounter
5. *one*: 1, a single unit	*won*: past tense of "to win"
6. *pain*: suffering	*pane*: sheet of glass or other substance
7. *passed*: past tense of "to pass"	*past*: gone by, ended, over
8. *peace*: calm	*piece*: section
9. *plain*: not beautiful; obvious	*plane*: airplane
10. *presence*: close proximity	*presents*: gifts
11. *principal*: main; head of a school	*principle*: rule
12. *quiet*: not noisy	*quite*: almost

Quick Quiz D

Directions: Match each word to its meaning. Write the letter of the meaning on the lines provided for you.

_____ **1.** peace

_____ **2.** plain

_____ **3.** pain

_____ **4.** pane

_____ **5.** plane

_____ **6.** meat

_____ **7.** lessen

_____ **8.** piece

_____ **9.** lesson

_____ **10.** meet

a. airplane

b. instruction

c. not beautiful; obvious

d. section

e. calm

f. encounter

g. suffering

h. to reduce

i. sheet of glass or other substance

j. animal flesh

Ten More Confusing Word Pairs

Rain is precipitation, water that comes from clouds to the sky. *Reign* is a monarch's rule. It is the government of a king or queen. Below are ten more confusing word pairs:

Word	Meaning
1. reed	plants
read	interpret the written word
2. right	correct
write	to form letters or symbols to create words, sentences, etc.
3. rote	memorize
wrote	past tense of "to write"
4. sail	travel by boat (verb), canvas sheet for collecting wind (noun)
sale	discount prices
5. see	to view (verb); diocese (noun)
sea	ocean
6. sew	work with needle and thread
so	consequently
7. shear	to cut
sheer	transparent
8. soul	conscience
sole	single
9. tail	hind part
tale	story
10. than	comparison
then	at that time

Spelling Essentials for the Pre-GED Student

Quick Quiz E

Directions: Write the definition of each of the following word pairs.

1. reed: _____

   read: _____

2. right: _____

   write: _____

3. sew: _____

   so: _____

4. see: _____

   sea: _____

5. rote: _____

   wrote: _____

6. sail: _____

   sale: _____

7. tail: _____

   tale: _____

8. shear: _____

   sheer: _____

9. soul: _____

   sole: _____

10. than: _____

   then: _____

Twelve *Final* Confusing Words

Their means "belonging to them." As you have already read, *they're* is a contraction for "they are." *There* indicates a place, as in "over there." Below are a dozen more confusing word pairs:

1. *to*: toward   *too*: also   *two*: 2

2. *through*: finished   *threw*: past tense of "to throw"

3. *vein*: blood vessel   *vane*: blade of a fan   *vain*: egotistical

4. *vial*: container   *vile*: horrid

5. *way*: means   *weigh*: to measure weight

6. *whine*: complain   *wine*: drink

7. *where*: in what direction   *wear*: erosion,
                                     to cover your body with clothing

8. *we're*: we are   *were*: past tense of "to be"

9. *witch*: crone   *which*: that one

10. *weak*: not strong   *week*: 7 days

11. *whether*: if   *weather*: atmospheric conditions

12. *wood*: lumber   *would*: could

Quick Quiz F

Directions: Circle the correct definition for each word in *italics*.

1. *whine*	complain	drink	horrid
2. *weak*	7 days	not strong	awful
3. *vein*	egotistical	blood vessel	blade of a fan
4. *which*	that one	crone	past tense of "to be"
5. *wood*	lumber	could	if
6. *wear*	means	erosion	we are

Answers to the Quick Quizzes

Answers to Quick Quiz A

1. four, for

2. phase, faze

3. faint, feint

4. fair, fare

5. flour, flower

6. guerrilla, gorilla

Answers to Quick Quiz B

1. *heard*: listened — *herd*: group of animals

2. *hall*: entryway — *haul*: to drag

3. *grate*: irritate, chop — *great*: large amount, enthusiastic, considerable, excellent

4. *hair*: fur — *heir*: beneficiary of an estate

5. *guilt*: blame — *gilt*: thin gold covering

Answers to Quick Quiz C

1. *leech*: bloodsucking worm

2. *hole*: crater

3. *here*: in this place

4. *hours*: 60 minutes

5. *knew*: past tense of "to know"

6. *hear*: listen

7. *whole*: entire

8. *ours*: belonging to you

9. *new*: not old

10. *leach*: to dissolve

Answers to Quick Quiz D

1. e

2. c

3. g

4. i

5. a

6. j

7. h

8. d

9. b

10. f

Answers to Quick Quiz E

1. *reed*: plants   *read*: interpret the written word

2. *right*: correct   *write*: to form letters

3. *sew*: work with needle and thread   *so*: consequently

4. *see*: to view (verb); diocese (noun) *sea*: ocean

5. *rote*: memorize   *wrote*: past tense of "to write"

6. *sail*: travel by boat (verb), canvas   *sale*: discount prices
sheet to collect wind (noun)

7. *tail*: hind part   *tale*: story

8. *shear*: to cut   *sheer*: transparent

9. *soul*: conscience   *sole:* single

10. *than*: comparison   *then*: at that time

Answers to Quick Quiz F

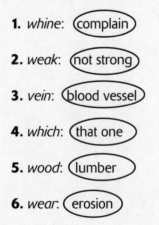

1. *whine*: complain

2. *weak*: not strong

3. *vein*: blood vessel

4. *which*: that one

5. *wood*: lumber

6. *wear*: erosion

Practice Test

Directions: Match each word to its meaning. Write the letter of the meaning on the lines provided for you.

_____ **1.** faint

_____ **2.** feint

_____ **3.** for

_____ **4.** four

_____ **5.** gorilla

_____ **6.** guerrilla

_____ **7.** guilt

_____ **8.** gilt

_____ **9.** heard

_____ **10.** herd

a. type of soldier

b. because

c. thin gold covering

d. group of animals

e. pass out

f. blame

g. trick

h. listened

i. ape

j. the number 4

Answers

1. e

2. g

3. b

4. j

5. i

6. a

7. f

8. c

9. h

10. d

Reevaluating Your Skills

Posttest

Take this posttest to see how much you learned. Use your results to focus on the sections of the book that you need to review the most.

Fundamentals of Spelling

Directions: Some of the following words are misspelled. Write **C** if the word is spelled correctly and write **X** if the word is spelled incorrectly. Then write the misspelled words correctly on the lines provided for you.

_____**1.** surprise

_____**2.** laughter

_____**3.** salmon

_____**4.** phonetic

_____**5.** photograph

_____**6.** biege

_____**7.** spagetti

_____**8.** raspberry

_____**9.** neumonia

_____**10.** psychology

_____**11.** anonymous

_____**12.** merchant

_____**13.** calender

_____**14.** judge

_____**15.** aisle

_____**16.** libberty

_____**17.** education

_____**18.** hospital

_____**19.** doller

_____**20.** gymnasium

Write the misspelled word correctly:

_____   _____

_____   _____

_____   _____

Spelling Rules

Directions: The words on the left are misspelled. The words on the right are spelled correctly. Match each misspelled word on the left to the correct spelling on the right. Write the letter of your answer on the lines provided for you.

_____**1.** memorys   **a.** friend

_____**2.** tragedys   **b.** neighbor

_____**3.** turkies   **c.** hopefully

_____**4.** Im   **d.** receive

_____**5.** hopfully   **e.** knives

_____**6.** fahrenheit   **f.** memories

_____**7.** veiws   **g.** quantity

_____**8.** cemetary   **h.** ninety-nine

_____**9.** qantity   **i.** I'm

_____**10.** recieve   **j.** weekday

_____**11.** mysterys   **k.** old-fashioned

_____**12.** oldfashioned   **l.** radios

_____**13.** ninetynine   **m.** views

_____**14.** nieghbor   **n.** tragedies

_____**15.** halfs   **o.** couldn't

_____**16.** week-day   **p.** Fahrenheit

_____**17.** knifs   **q.** mysteries

_____**18.** freind   **r.** halves

_____**19.** radioes   **s.** turkeys

_____**20.** couldnt   **t.** cemetery

Putting the Words Together

Directions: In each of the following groups of words, only one of the words is misspelled. Choose the misspelled word and spell it correctly on the lines provided for you.

_____ **1.** incredible   prototype   autamobile

_____ **2.** capital   telascope   pseudonym

_____ **3.** chronacle   biology   sympathy

_____ **4.** horoscope   democracy   fatory

_____ **5.** autobiographie   perfect   defect

_____ **6.** sychology   magnify   integrity

_____ **7.** scrible   contact   abbreviation

_____ **8.** terminal   sause   sausage

_____ **9.** salary   mispell   ultramarine

_____ **10.** premature   parograph   hypocrisy

_____ **11.** reapear   demolish   epidemic

_____ **12.** autograph   geography   bycycle

_____ **13.** Pentagon   neighborhood   sking

_____ **14.** November   ponies   carful

_____ **15.** decade   holy   truely

Words Commonly Confused

Directions: Some of the following words are misspelled. Write **C** if the word is spelled correctly and write **X** if it is spelled incorrectly. Then write the words correctly on the lines provided for you.

_____ **1.** umbrella

_____ **2.** anser

_____ **3.** hundred

_____ **4.** guess

_____ **5.** beootiful

_____ **6.** ache

_____ **7.** crowd

_____ **8.** right

_____ **9.** weether

_____ **10.** flour

_____ **11.** diamond

_____ **12.** disappear

_____ **13.** Capitol

_____ **14.** eigth

_____ **15.** deside

_____ **16.** gorilla

_____ **17.** its'

_____ **18.** whether

_____ **19.** flower

_____ **20.** business

Write the misspelled words correctly:

_____   _____

_____   _____

_____   _____

Wrapping It All Up

Directions: In each of the following groups of words, only one of the words is misspelled. Choose the misspelled word and spell it correctly on the lines provided for you.

_____ **1.** freind   enemies   holidays

_____ **2.** hopefully   youre   old-fashioned

_____ **3.** neighbor   wekday   ninety-nine

_____ **4.** wed'   quantity   memories

_____ **5.** taxs   terminal   sauce

_____ **6.** autobiography   mysteries   wel'l

_____ **7.** receive   boxxes   peaches

_____ **8.** autocratic   sausage   turkies

_____ **9.** automatic   halves   would'nt

_____ **10.** autopsy   cemetery   knifes

_____ **11.** weren't   veiws   tragedies

_____ **12.** memorys   recover   disagree

_____ **13.** atypical   Febuary   holiday

_____ **14.** coworker   across   mariage

_____ **15.** December   many   salery

_____ **16.** November   sincerly   forward

_____ **17.** Sepember   vegetable   perfect

_____ **18.** lable   Illinois   exit

_____ **19.** magnet   its   Wenesday

_____ **20.** whether   Im   bore

Answers to Fundamentals of Spelling

C **1.** surprise

C **2.** laughter

C **3.** salmon

C **4.** phonetic

C **5.** photograph

X **6.** biege

X **7.** spagetti

C **8.** raspberry

X **9.** neumonia

C **10.** psychology

C **11.** anonymous

C **12.** merchant

X **13.** calender

C **14.** judge

C **15.** aisle

X **16.** libberty

C **17.** education

C **18.** hospital

X **19.** doller

C **20.** gymnasium

Misspelled Words Corrected

6. beige

7. spaghetti

9. pneumonia

13. calendar

16. liberty

19. dollar

Answers to Spelling Rules

1. f
2. n
3. s
4. i
5. c
6. p
7. m
8. t
9. g
10. d
11. q
12. k
13. h
14. b
15. r
16. j
17. e
18. a
19. l
20. o

Answers to Putting the Words Together

1. automobile
2. telescope
3. chronicle
4. factory
5. autobiography
6. psychology
7. scribble
8. sauce
9. misspell
10. paragraph
11. reappear
12. bicycle
13. skiing
14. careful
15. truly

Answers to Words Commonly Confused

C **1.** umbrella

X **2.** anser

C **3.** hundred

C **4.** guess

X **5.** beootiful

C **6.** ache

C **7.** crowd

C **8.** right

X **9.** weether

C **10.** flour

C **11.** diamond

C **12.** disappear

C **13.** Capitol

X **14.** eigth

X **15.** deside

C **16.** gorilla

X **17.** its'

C **18.** whether

C **19.** flower

C **20.** business

Misspelled Words Corrected

2. answer

5. beautiful

9. weather

14. eighth

15. decide

17. it's

Answers to Wrapping It All Up

1. friend
2. you're
3. weekday
4. we'd
5. taxes
6. we'll
7. boxes
8. turkeys
9. wouldn't
10. knives
11. views
12. memories
13. February
14. marriage
15. salary
16. sincerely
17. September
18. label
19. Wednesday
20. I'm

Appendices

Word Parts A

In Section IV, we learned about prefixes, roots, and suffixes—in other words, *word parts*. This list has some of the common prefixes, roots, and suffixes that make up the building blocks of numerous English words. You should read through this list carefully and come back to it every now and then to jump-start your memory.

Prefixes

Prefix	Meaning	Example
a-	in, on, of, to	*abed*—in bed
a-, ab-, abs-	from, away	*abrade*—wear off
		absent—away, not present
a-, an-	lacking, not	*asymptomatic*—showing no symptoms
		anaerobic—able to live without air
ac-, ad-, af-, ag-, al-, an-, ap-, ar-, as-, at-	to, toward	*accost*—approach and speak to
		adjunct—something added to
		aggregate—bring together
ambi-, amphi-	around, both	*ambidextrous*—using both hands equally
		amphibious—living both in water and on land
ana-	up, again, anew, throughout	*analyze*—loosen up, break up into parts
		anagram—word spelled by mixing up letters of another word
ante-	before	*antediluvian*—before the Flood

213

Prefix	Meaning	Example
anti-	against	*antiwar*—against war
arch-	first, chief	*archetype*—first model
auto-	self	*automobile*—self-moving vehicle
bene-, ben-	good, well	*benefactor*—one who does good deeds
bi-	two	*bilateral*—two-sided
circum-	around	*circumnavigate*—sail around
com-, co-, col-, con-, cor-	with, together	*concentrate*—bring closer together
		cooperate—work with
		collapse—fall together
contra-, contro-, counter-	against	*contradict*—speak against
		counterclockwise—against the clock
de-	away from, down, opposite of	*detract*—draw away from
demi-	half	*demitasse*—half cup
di-	twice, double	*dichromatic*—having two colors
dia-	across, through	*diameter*—measurement across
dis-, di-	not, away from	*dislike*—to not like
		digress—turn away from the subject
dys-	bad, poor	*dyslexia*—poor reading
equi-	equal	*equivalent*—of equal value
ex-, e-, ef-	from, out	*expatriate*—one who lives outside his or her native country
		emit—send out
extra-	outside, beyond	*extraterrestrial*—from beyond Earth
fore-	in front of, previous	*forecast*—tell ahead of time
		foreleg—front leg
geo-	earth	*geography*—science of the earth's surface
homo-	same, like	*homophonic*—sounding the same
hyper-	too much, over	*hyperactive*—overly active
hypo-	too little, under	*hypothermia*—state of having too little body heat

Prefix	Meaning	Example
in-, il-, ig-, im-, ir-	not	*innocent*—not guilty
		ignorant—not knowing
		illogical—not logical
		irresponsible—not responsible
in-, il-, im-, ir-	on, into, in	*impose*—place on
		invade—go into
intra-, intro-	within, inside	*intrastate*—within a state
inter-	between, among	*interplanetary*—between planets
mal-, male-	bad, wrong, poor	*maladjust*—adjust poorly
		malevolent—ill-wishing
mis-	badly, wrongly	*misunderstand*—understand wrongly
mis-, miso-	hatred	*misogyny*—hatred of women
mono-	single, one	*monorail*—train that runs on a single rail
neo-	new	*neolithic*—of the New Stone Age
non-	not	*nonentity*—a person or thing of little or no importance
ob-	over, against, toward	*obstruct*—stand against
omni-	all	*omnipresent*—present in all places
pan-	all	*panorama*—a complete view
peri-	around, near	*periscope*—device for seeing all around
poly-	many	*polygonal*—many-sided
post-	after	*postmortem*—after death
pre-	before, earlier than	*prejudice*—judgment in advance
pro-	in favor of, forward, in front of	*proceed*—go forward
		prowar—in favor of war
re-	back, again	*rethink*—think again
		reimburse—pay back
retro-	backward	*retrospective*—looking backward
se-	apart, away	*seclude*—keep away
semi-	half	*semiconscious*—half conscious
sub-, suc-, suf-,	under, beneath	*subscribe*—write underneath

Prefix	Meaning	Example
sug, sus-		*suspend*—hang down
		suffer—undergo
super-	above, greater	*superfluous*—overflowing, beyond what is needed
syn-, sym-, syl-, sys-	with, at the same time	*synthesis*—a putting together
		sympathy—a feeling with
tele-	far	*television*—machine for seeing far
trans-	across	*transport*—carry across a distance
un-	not	*uninformed*—not informed
vice-	acting for, next in rank to	*viceroy*—one acting for the king

Roots

Root	Meaning	Examples
acr	bitter	*acrid, acrimony*
act, ag	do, act, drive	*action, react, agitate*
acu	sharp, keen	*acute, acumen*
agog	leader	*pedagogue, demagogic*
agr	field	*agronomy, agriculture*
ali	other	*alias, alienate, inalienable*
alt	high	*altitude, contralto*
alter, altr	other, change	*alternative, altercation, altruism*
am, amic	love, friend	*amorous, amiable*
anim	mind, life, spirit	*animism, animate, animosity*
annu, enni	year	*annual, superannuated, biennial*
anthrop	man	*anthropoid, misanthropy*
apt, ept	fit	*apt, adapt, ineptitude*
aqu	water	*aquatic, aquamarine*
arbit	judge	*arbiter, arbitrary*
arch	chief	*anarchy, matriarch*
arm	arm, weapon	*army, armature, disarm*
art	skill, a fitting together	*artisan, artifact, articulate*
aster, astr	star	*asteroid, disaster, astral*
aud, audit, aur	hear	*auditorium, audition, auricle*
aur	gold	*aureate, aureomycin*
aut	self	*autism, autograph*
bell	war	*antebellum, belligerent*
ben, bene	well, good	*benevolent, benefit*
bibli	book	*bibliography, bibliophile*
bio	life	*biosphere, amphibious*
brev	short	*brevity, abbreviation*
cad, cas, cid	fall	*cadence, casualty, occasion, accident*
cand	white, shining	*candid, candle, incandescent*
cant, chant	sing, charm	*cantor, recant, enchant*
cap, capt, cept, cip	take, seize, hold	*capable, captive, accept, incipient*

Root	Meaning	Examples
capit	head	*capital, decapitate, recapitulate*
carn	flesh	*carnal, incarnate*
cede, ceed, cess	go, yield	*secede, exceed, process*
cent	hundred	*percentage, centimeter*
cern, cert	perceive, make certain, decide	*concern, certificate, certain*
chrom	color	*monochrome, chromatic*
chron	time	*chronometer, anachronism*
cide, cis	cut, kill	*genocide, incision*
cit	summon, impel	*cite, excite, incitement*
civ	citizen	*uncivil, civilization*
clam, claim	shout	*clamorous, proclaim, claimant*
clar	clear	*clarity, clarion, declare*
clin	slope, lean	*inclination, recline*
clud, clus, clos	close, shut	*seclude, recluse, closet*
cogn	know	*recognize, incognito*
col, cul	till	*colony, cultivate, agriculture*
corp	body	*incorporate, corpse*
cosm	order, world	*cosmetic, cosmos, cosmopolitan*
crac, crat	power, rule	*democrat, theocracy*
cre, cresc, cret	grow	*increase, crescent, accretion*
cred	trust, believe	*credit, incredible*
crux, cruc	cross	*crux, crucial, crucifix*
crypt	hidden	*cryptic, cryptography*
culp	blame	*culprit, culpability*
cur, curr, curs	run, course	*occur, current, incursion*
cura	care	*curator, accurate*
cycl	wheel, circle	*bicycle, cyclone*
dec	ten	*decade, decimal*
dem	people	*demographic, demagogue*
dent	tooth	*dental, indentation*
derm	skin	*dermatitis, pachyderm*
di, dia	day	*diary, quotidian*
dic, dict	say, speak	*indicative, edict, dictation*
dign	worthy	*dignified, dignitary*

Root	Meaning	Examples
doc, doct	teach, prove	*indoctrinate, docile, doctor*
domin	rule	*predominate, domineer, dominion*
dorm	sleep	*dormitory, dormant*
du	two	*duo, duplicity, dual*
duc, duct	lead	*educate, abduct, ductile*
dur	hard, lasting	*endure, obdurate, duration*
dyn	force, power	*dynamo, dynamite*
ego	I	*egomania, egotist*
equ	equal	*equation, equitable*
erg, urg	work, power	*energetic, metallurgy*
err	wander	*error, aberrant*
ev	time, age	*coeval, longevity*
fac, fact, fect, fic	do, make	*facility, factual, perfect, artifice*
fer	bear, carry	*prefer, refer, conifer, fertility*
ferv	boil	*fervid, effervesce*
fid	belief, faith	*infidelity, confidant, perfidious*
fin	end, limit	*finite, confine*
firm	strong	*reaffirm, infirmity*
flect, flex	bend	*reflex, inflection*
flor	flower	*florescent, floral*
flu, fluct, flux	flow	*fluid, fluctuation, influx*
form	shape	*formative, reform, formation*
fort	strong	*effort, fortitude*
frag, fract	break	*fragility, infraction*
fug	flee	*refuge, fugitive*
fus	pour, join	*infuse, transfusion*
gam	marry	*exogamy, polygamous*
ge, geo	earth	*geology, geode, perigee*
gen	birth, kind, race	*engender, general, generation*
gest	carry, bear	*gestation, ingest, digest*
gon	angle	*hexagonal, trigonometry*
grad, gress	step, go	*regress, gradation*
gram	writing	*grammar, cryptogram*
graph	writing	*telegraph, graphics*

Root	Meaning	Examples
grat	pleasing, agreeable	congratulate, gratuitous
grav	weight, heavy	gravity
greg	flock, crowd	gregarious, segregate
habit, hibit	have, hold	habitation, inhibit, habitual
heli	sun	helium, heliocentric, aphelion
hem	blood	hemoglobin, hemorrhage
her, hes	stick, cling	adherent, cohesive
hydr	water	dehydration, hydrofoil
iatr	heal, cure	pediatrics, psychiatry
iso	same, equal	isotope, isometric
it	journey, go	itinerary, exit
ject	throw	reject, subjective, projection
jud	judge	judicial, adjudicate
jug, junct	join	conjugal, juncture, conjunction
jur	swear	perjure, jurisprudence
labor	work	laborious, belabor
leg	law	legal, illegitimate
leg, lig, lect	choose, gather, read	illegible, eligible, select, lecture
lev	light, rise	levity, alleviate
liber	free	liberal, libertine
liter	letter	literate, alliterative
lith	rock, stone	neolithic, lithograph
loc	place	locale, locus, allocate
log	word, study	logic, biology, dialogue
loqu, locut	talk, speech	colloquial, loquacious, interlocutor
luc, lum	light	translucent, pellucid, illumine, luminous
lud, lus	play	allusion, ludicrous, interlude
magn	large, great	magnificent, magnitude
mal	bad, ill	malodorous, malinger
man, manu	hand	manifest, manicure, manuscript
mar	sea	maritime, submarine
mater, matr	mother	matriarchal, maternal
medi	middle	intermediary, medieval
mega	large, million	megaphone, megacycle

Root	Meaning	Examples
ment	mind	*demented, mental*
merg, mers	plunge, dip	*emerge, submersion*
meter, metr, mens	measure	*chronometer, metronome, geometry, commensurate*
micr	small	*microfilm, micron*
min	little	*minimum, minute*
mit, miss	send	*remit, admission, missive*
mon, monit	warn	*admonish, monument, monitor*
mor	custom	*mores, immoral*
mor, mort	death	*mortify, mortician*
morph	shape	*amorphous, anthropomorphic*
mov, mob, mot	move	*removal, automobile, motility*
multi	many	*multiply, multinational*
mut	change	*mutable, transmute*
nasc, nat	born	*native, natural, nascent, innate*
nav	ship, sail	*navy, navigable*
necr	dead, die	*necropolis, necrosis*
neg	deny	*renege, negative*
neo	new	*neologism, neoclassical*
nomen, nomin	name	*nomenclature, cognomen, nominate*
nomy	law, rule	*astronomy, antinomy*
nov	new	*novice, innovation*
ocul	eye	*binocular, oculist*
omni	all	*omniscient, omnibus*
onym	name	*pseudonym, eponymous*
oper	work	*operate, cooperation, inoperable*
ora	speak, pray	*oracle, oratory*
orn	decorate	*adorn, ornate*
orth	straight, correct	*orthodox, orthopedic*
pan	all	*panacea, pantheon*
pater, patr	father	*patriot, paternity*
path, pat, pass	feel, suffer	*telepathy, patient, compassion, passion*
ped	child	*pedagogue, pediatrics*

Root	Meaning	Examples
ped, pod	foot	pedestrian, impede, tripod
pel, puls	drive, push	impel, propulsion
pend, pens	hang	pendulous, suspense
pet, peat	seek	petition, impetus, repeat
phil	love	philosopher, Anglophile
phob	fear	phobic, agoraphobia
phon	sound	phonograph, symphony
phor	bearing	semaphore, metaphor
phot	light	photograph, photoelectric
pon, pos	place, put	component, repose, postpone
port	carry	report, portable, deportation
pot	power	potency, potential
press	press	pressure, impression
prim	first	primal, primordial
proto, prot	first	proton, protagonist
psych	mind	psychic, metempsychosis
pyr	fire	pyrite, pyrophobia
quer, quir, quis, ques	ask, seek	query, inquiry, inquisitive, quest
reg, rig, rect	straight, rule	regulate, dirigible, corrective
rid, ris	laugh	deride, risible, ridiculous
rog	ask	rogation, interrogate
rupt	break	erupt, interruption, rupture
sanct	holy	sacrosanct, sanctify, sanction
sci, scio	know	nescient, conscious, omniscience
scop	watch, view	horoscope, telescopic
scrib, script	write	scribble, proscribe, description
sed, sid, sess	sit, seat	sedate, residence, session
seg, sect	cut	segment, section, intersect
sent, sens	feel, think	nonsense, sensitive, sentient, dissent
sequ, secut	follow	sequel, consequence, consecutive
sign	sign, mark	signature, designate, assign
sol	alone	solitary, solo, desolate
solv, solu, solut	loosen	dissolve, soluble, absolution

Root	Meaning	Examples
somn	sleep	*insomnia, somnolent*
son	sound	*sonorous, unison*
soph	wise, wisdom	*philosophy, sophisticated*
spec, spic, spect	look	*specimen, conspicuous, spectacle*
spir	breathe	*spirit, conspire, respiration*
stab, stat	stand	*unstable, status, station, establish*
stead	place	*instead, steadfast*
string, strict	bind	*astringent, stricture, restrict*
stru, struct	build	*construe, structure, destructive*
sum, sumpt	take	*presume, consumer, assumption*
tang, ting, tact, tig	touch	*tangent, contingency, contact, tactile, contiguous*
tax, tac	arrange, arrangement	*taxonomy, tactic*
techn	skill, art	*technique, technician*
tele	far	*teletype, telekinesis*
tempor	time	*temporize, extemporaneous*
ten, tain, tent	hold	*tenant, tenacity, retention, contain*
tend, tens, tent	stretch	*contend, extensive, intent*
tenu	thin	*tenuous, attenuate*
term	end	*terminal, terminate*
terr, ter	land, earth	*inter, terrain*
test	witness	*attest, testify*
the	god	*polytheism, theologist*
therm	heat	*thermos, isotherm*
tom	cut	*atomic, appendectomy*
tort, tors	twist	*tortuous, torsion, contort*
tract	pull, draw	*traction, attract, protract*
trib	assign, pay	*attribute, tribute, retribution*
trud, trus	thrust	*obtrude, intrusive*
turb	agitate	*perturb, turbulent, disturb*
umbr	shade	*umbrella, penumbra, umbrage*
uni	one	*unify, disunity, union*
urb	city	*urbane, suburb*

Root	Meaning	Examples
vac	empty	*vacuous, evacuation*
vad, vas	go	*invade, evasive*
val, vail	strength, worth	*valid, avail, prevalent*
ven, vent	come	*advent, convene, prevention*
ver	true	*aver, veracity, verity*
verb	word	*verbose, adverb, verbatim*
vert, vers	turn	*revert, perversion*
vest	dress	*vestment*
vid, vis	see	*video, evidence, vision, revise*
vinc, vict	conquer	*evince, convict, victim*
viv, vit	life	*vivid, revive, vital*
voc, vok	call	*vociferous, provocative, revoke*
vol	wish	*involuntary, volition*
voly, volut	roll, turn	*involve, convoluted, revolution*
vulg	common	*divulge, vulgarity*
zo	animal	*zoologist, paleozoic*

Suffixes

Suffix	Meaning	Example
-able, -ble	able, capable	*acceptable*—able to be accepted
-acious, -cious	characterized by, having the quality of	*fallacious*—having the quality of a fallacy
-age	sum, total	*mileage*—total number of miles
-al	of, like, suitable for	*theatrical*—suitable for theater
-ance, -ancy	act or state of	*disturbance*—act of disturbing
-ant, -ent	one who	*defendant*—one who defends himself or herself
-ary, -ar	having the nature of, concerning	*military*—relating to soldiers
		polar—concerning the pole
-cy	act, state, or position of	*presidency*—position of president
		ascendancy—state of being raised up
-dom	state, rank, that which belongs to	*wisdom*—state of being wise
-ence	act, state, or quality of	*dependence*—state of depending
-er, -or	one who, that which	*doer*—one who does
		conductor—that which conducts
-escent	becoming	*obsolescent*—becoming obsolete
-fy	to make	*pacify*—make peaceful
-hood	state, condition	*adulthood*—state of being adult
-ic, -ac	of, like	*demonic*—of or like a demon
-il, -ile	having to do with, like, suitable for	*civil*—having to do with citizens
		tactile—having to do with touch
-ion	act or condition of	*operation*—act of operating
-ious	having, characterized by	*anxious*—characterized by anxiety
-ish	like, somewhat	*foolish*—like a fool
-ism	belief or practice of	*racism*—belief in racial superiority
-ist	one who does, makes, or is concerned with	*scientist*—one concerned with science

Suffix	Meaning	Example
-ity, -ty, -y	character or state of being	*amity*—friendship
		jealousy—state of being jealous
-ive	of, relating to, tending to	*destructive*—tending to destroy
-logue, -loquy	speech or writing	*monologue*—speech by one person
		colloquy—conversation
-logy	speech, study of	*geology*—study of the earth
-ment	act or state of	*abandonment*—act of abandoning
-mony	a resulting thing, condition, or state	*patrimony*—property inherited from one's father
-ness	act or quality	*kindness*—quality of being kind
-ory	having the quality of; a place or thing for	*compensatory*—having the quality of a compensation
		lavatory—place for washing
-ous, -ose	full of, having	*glamorous*—full of glamour
-ship	skill, state of being	*horsemanship*—skill in riding
		ownership—state of being an owner
-some	full of, like	*frolicsome*—playful
-tude	state or quality of	*rectitude*—state of being morally upright
-ward	in the direction of	*homeward*—in the direction of home
-y	full of, like, somewhat	*wily*—full of wiles

Spelling Essentials for the Pre-GED Student

About the GED B

What to Expect on the GED

There are five GED tests:

- Language Arts, Writing
- Mathematics
- Science
- Social Studies
- Language Arts, Reading

On every test (except for Language Arts, Writing) all the questions will be multiple choice. Each multiple-choice question will have five possible answer choices. For each question, you must choose the best answer of the five possible choices. The multiple-choice questions may be based on a graphic, a text, or a mathematics problem, or they may just test your knowledge of a particular subject. Let's take a look at the kinds of questions asked on each subject area test.

Language Arts, Writing

The multiple-choice section of the Writing exam tests English grammar and usage. It contains several passages and questions about those passages in which you find errors or determine the best way to rewrite particular sentences. The essay section will require you to write a 200- to 250-word essay on a particular topic in 45 minutes. This question won't test your knowledge of a particular subject, such as the War of 1812 or the Pythagorean Theorem. Instead, you will write about your own life experiences. The readers of the essay will not be grading the essay based on how much you know or don't know about the topic, but rather on how well you use standard English.

Social Studies

The Social Studies Test contains multiple-choice questions on history, economics, political science, and geography. In the United States, the test focuses on U.S. history and government, while the test in Canada focuses on Canadian history and government. World history will be included, too. Some of the questions will be based on reading passages, and some questions will be based on graphics such as maps, charts, illustrations, or political cartoons.

Science

The Science Test contains multiple-choice questions on physical and life sciences. You will also see questions on earth science, space science, life science, health science, and environmental science. As with the Social Studies Test, some of the Science questions will be based upon reading passages and some of the questions will be based upon graphics such as scientific diagrams.

Language Arts, Reading

The Language Arts, Reading Test is similar to the Social Studies and Science Tests in that the multiple-choice questions will be based on passages. The questions will be based on longer passages than questions in the other subject area tests. In the Language Arts, Reading Test, some of the questions will be based on a poem, some on prose, some on a piece of drama, and some on documents that you might encounter in the workplace.

Mathematics

There are two parts to the Mathematics Test. You can use a calculator on Part I, but not on Part II. The Mathematics Test uses multiple-choice questions to measure your skills in arithmetic, algebra, geometry, and problem solving. Some of the questions will ask you to find the answer to a problem, while others will require you to find the best way to solve the problem. Many of the questions will be based upon diagrams. Some of the questions will be grouped into sets that require you to draw upon information from a number of sources, such as graphs and charts.

The majority of GED questions on all five of the tests measure your skills and test-taking abilities. What does this mean for you? This means that if you work hard to sharpen your test-taking skills, you will be much more prepared for success on the tests than if you sat down and memorized names, dates, facts, properties, charts, or other bits of information. Basically, you will have more success on the GED if you know how to take the tests than if all you know is information about reading, writing, science, social studies, and math. Let's look at some strategies for answering multiple-choice questions.

Answering Multiple-Choice Questions

The key to success on multiple-choice tests is understanding the questions and how to find the correct answer. Each multiple-choice question on the GED will be followed by five answer choices: (1), (2), (3), (4), and (5). There will be no trick questions and no questions intended to confuse you. If you use the strategies that follow, you will be successful on the multiple-choice questions.

Strategies for Answering Multiple-Choice Questions

- **Read the question carefully and make sure you know what it is asking.** Read each question slowly. If you rush through the question, you might miss a key word that could cost you the correct answer. You might want to run your pencil under the question as you read it to be sure that you don't miss anything in the question. If you don't understand the question after the first time you read it, go back and read it another time or two until you do understand it.

- **Don't overanalyze the question or read something into the question that just isn't there.** Many test-takers make the mistake of overanalyzing questions, looking for some trick or hidden meaning that the test-creators added for the sake of confusion. The GED Test-creators didn't do that on any of the questions, so take each question at face value. Each question will say exactly what it means, so don't try to interpret something that isn't there.

- **Circle or underline the key words in the question.** As you read through the question, locate any important words in the question and either circle or underline the word or words. Important words will be anything taken directly from the chart, table, graph, or reading passage on which the question is based. Other important words will be words like *compare, contrast, similar, different,* or *main idea.* By circling or underlining the key words, you will understand the question better and will be more prepared to recognize the correct answer.

- **After you read the question, try to answer the question in your head before you look at the answer choices.** If you think you know the answer to the question without even looking at the answer choices, then you most likely will recognize the correct answer right away when you read the possible answer choices. Also, if you think you know the correct answer right away, then you should be very confident in your answer when you find it listed among the possible answer choices.

- **Try covering the answer choices while you are reading the question.** To try answering the question in your head without being influenced by the answer choices, cover the answer choices with your hand as you read the question. This technique will also help prevent you from reading something into the question that isn't there based on something you saw in one of the answer choices first. Covering the answer choices may also help you concentrate only on the question to make sure you read it carefully and correctly.

- **Carefully read all the answer choices before answering the question.** You need to look at all the possibilities before you choose the best or correct answer. Even if you think you know the answer before looking at the possible answer choices, read all of the answer choices anyway. If you read through two of the answer choices and you find that choice (3) is a good answer, keep reading because (4) or (5) may very well be a better answer. Finally, by reading all the answer choices, you can be more confident in your answer because you will see that the other choices are definitely incorrect.

- **Eliminate answer choices that you know are wrong.** As you read through all the choices, some will obviously be incorrect. When you find those answer choices, mark through them. This will help you narrow the possible choices. In addition, marking through incorrect answers will prevent you from choosing an incorrect answer by mistake.

- **Don't spend too much time on one question.** If you read a question and you just can't seem to find the best or correct answer, circle the question, skip it, and come back to it later. Your time will be better spent on questions that you can answer. Your time is limited, so don't struggle with one question if you could correctly answer three others in the same amount of time.

- **Go with your first answer.** Once you choose an answer, stick to it. A test-taker's first hunch is usually the correct one. There is a reason why your brain told you to choose a particular answer, so stand by it. Also, don't waste time debating over whether the answer you chose is correct. Go with your first answer and move on.

- **Don't go back and change your answer unless you have a good, solid reason to do so.** Remember that your first hunch is usually the best, so don't change your answer on a whim. One of the only times you should change your answer on a previous question is if you find something later in the test that contradicts what you chose. The only other time you should change an answer is if you remember very clearly a teacher's lecture, a reading passage, or some other reliable source of information to the contrary of what you chose.

- **Look for hints within the answer choices.** For example, some sets of answer choices may contain two choices that vary by only a word or two. Chances are that the correct answer is one of those two answers.

- **Watch out for absolutes.** Other hints within answer choices can be words called absolutes. These words include *always, never, only,* or *completely*. These words severely limit the possibility of that answer choice being right because the absolutes make answer choices that include them correct under certain, very limited circumstances.

- **If you just don't know the correct answer, guess.** That's right, guess. The GED Tests are scored based on how many questions you answer correctly, and there is no point penalty for answering incorrectly. Therefore, why leave questions unanswered? If you do, you have no chance at getting any points for those. However, if you guess, you at least have a chance to get some points. Before you guess, try to eliminate as many wrong answer choices as possible. You have a much greater chance of choosing the correct answer if you can weed out some that are incorrect. This strategy is especially helpful if you have several questions left for which you are going to guess.

- **Be aware of how much time you have left on the test.** However, don't glance down at your watch or up at the clock after every question to check the time. You will be instructed at the beginning of the test as to the amount of time you have to complete the test. Just be aware of that amount of time. The creators of the GED Tests designed the tests and the test times so that you will have ample time to complete the tests. As you approach the point at which you have 10 minutes left, make sure that you are not spending your time answering the difficult questions if you still have other questions ahead of you that you can answer. If you have answered all the questions that you can with relatively little difficulty, go back and work on those that gave you trouble. If you come down to the wire and have a few left, guess at the answers. There is no penalty for wrong answers on the GED.

- **If you have time left at the end of the test, go back to any questions that you skipped.** As you just read, after you finish all the questions that you can without too much difficulty, you should go back over the test and find the ones you skipped. The amount of time you have left should determine the amount of time you spend on each unanswered question. For example, if you have 10 questions left and 10 minutes left, try to work on a few of them. However, if you have 10 questions left and 2 minutes left, go through and guess on each of the remaining questions.

What's Next?

Working with this book is the first step toward getting your GED. But what should you do next? Many people find it helpful to take a GED test-preparation course. Call your local high school counselor or the Adult Education or Continuing Education Department at your local community college, college, or university. The people in those offices can tell you where courses are offered and how to enroll. In addition to taking a GED course, continue studying on your own with this book and others in the ARCO line of books.

Once you feel ready to take the tests, contact the GED Testing Service to find out when and where the exams will be administered next:

General Educational Development
GED Testing Service
American Council on Education
One Dupont Circle, NW
Washington, D.C. 20036
Phone: 800-626-9433 (toll-free)
Web site: www.gedtest.org

Good luck!

Test-Taking Tips and Strategies C

I. Prepare Your Mind

Being mentally ready to take a test is very important. You must walk into any test with a positive mental attitude. YOU CAN DO IT!

This should be easy. You've studied this book, and maybe others. You're comfortable with the material on the test. You won't run into any surprises. So take some deep breaths and walk into the test room knowing that you can succeed!

Be relaxed. Be confident.

II. The Night Before

Cramming doesn't work for any kind of test. So the night before the test, you should briefly review some of the concepts that you're still unsure of. Then go straight to bed. Make sure you get enough sleep. You'll be glad you did the next morning.

III. The Morning of the Test

Did you know that you think better when you have a full stomach? So don't skip breakfast the morning of the test. Get to your test site early (you should make a practice run before the test if the test site is in an unfamiliar area).

Come prepared with all the materials you'll need. These might include number 2 pencils or identification. You might want to wear a watch too, in case the room you're in doesn't have a clock.

IV. Test Time

Before the test begins, make sure you have everything you need. This will keep your test anxiety low.

Choose a comfortable seat (if possible!) in a spot where you will not be distracted, cold, hot, etc.

Try not to talk to other test-takers before the test. Anxiety is contagious.

V. Managing Time

Scan through the test quickly before starting it. Be familiar with the time for each section and the time the test should be over. Look at how many questions there are, and where the answers are filled in.

READ ALL DIRECTIONS VERY CAREFULLY.

VI. Know your Test

On the GED, test questions are arranged in order of difficulty. This means the easier questions come first. So the more time you spend on the easier early questions, the less time you'll have for the harder questions later in the section. If you're stuck, don't get worried or frustrated. Circle the question and move on. Go back to it later, once you've finished the rest of the test. And make sure that you skip space on the answer documents for every question you skip on the test.

VII. Test Review

Once you've finished taking the test, look back over the exam to review what you've done. Resist the urge to run away as fast as you can once you mark your last answer. Some things to look for:

Make sure you've answered all the questions.

Proofread (when you're doing any written work).

Check your math for careless mistakes (when you're doing any math sections).

Answer any questions you skipped.

Good luck!